cute croc...

for tiny tots

cute crochet
for tiny tots
25 modern designs for babies and toddlers

Helen Ardley

hamlyn

For my daughter, Lauren, who is the inspiration behind the designs and the reason
I wrote the book in the first place.

First published in Great Britain in 2006 by Hamlyn,
a division of Octopus Publishing Group Ltd
2–4 Heron Quays, London E14 4JP

ISBN-13: 978-0-600-61425-8
ISBN-10: 0-600-61425-5

A CIP catalogue record for this book is available from the British Library

Printed and bound in China

10 9 8 7 6 5 4 3 2 1

Note
Keep all small items used in the projects in this book, such as beads and sequins, out
of reach of young children.

contents

introduction

I have really enjoyed designing the garments, accessories and soft furnishings in this book, and I hope I've included colours and textures that will appeal to the mums and dads, family and friends of every baby and toddler.

There are hats and scarves, sweaters and cardigans for every occasion. Mittens and bootees for newborns are made in the softest of yarns to keep tiny toes and delicate fingers snug and warm. A floppity teddy and dress-up rag doll will quickly become firm favourites with any little one to cuddle and play with.

Today, bedrooms for babies and toddlers are bright and colourful, so I have included accessories to make these rooms fun for children. There are super storage pockets to fill with toys, a wonderfully comfortable floor cushion and hanging motifs with extra special detailing.

The patterns range from the very simple to moderately challenging, so there is something here for beginner and experienced crocheter alike. Everything is fun to make, and you can adapt any of the designs by changing the colours to suit your child or your decor.

I hope you have as much fun making these garments and accessories as I did designing them.

Happy crocheting!

yarns

The days when the only yarns available for babies and toddlers were pastel shades of pink and blue are long gone. Now it is possible to buy a range of natural and synthetic yarns in a rainbow of pretty colours.

yarn types

Wherever possible, buy the yarn brand recommended in the patterns. These are the yarns used to make the garments and items shown in the photographs, and they are certain to give the desired results in terms of size, tension and finished appearance.

Because comfort is a top priority for clothes for babies and toddlers, cotton yarns feature prominently in these designs. They are soft enough for children's sensitive skins, they aren't scratchy, and they are ideal for wearing all year round – warm in winter and cool in summer.

Before you begin work, think about the qualities of the yarn you intend to use. Synthetic yarns may be easy to wash, but natural fibres maintain their

shape for many years and often get better with age. Items in natural fibres can be passed down to a new sibling and still look good.

yarn and dye lots

Yarn is dyed in batches, and dye lots can vary greatly. When you are buying always check the dye lot number on the yarn labels to make sure that you use balls from the same dye lot for the main colour of your project, otherwise you run the risk of a jacket or jumper being unintentionally stripy.

substituting yarn

If you want to crochet with different yarns from those specified in the patterns, please remember to think about the stitch size and the weight of the yarn. A yarn might crochet up to the right number of stitches and rows to the centimetre (inch), but the resulting fabric may be so heavy that it pulls the design out of shape. Before you use a different yarn, crochet a tension (gauge) square to check the stitch size and then see if you like the feel of the fabric. Cotton yarn is heavier than wool and is less elastic when it is crocheted, so always check the tension before you change yarns from those stated in the pattern.

Even when you use the yarn specified it is worth checking the tension before you begin, because your crochet might be tighter or looser than mine. As with knitting, it is possible to adjust tension slightly by using a smaller or larger hook, and the few minutes it will take to crochet a small square or circle will never be wasted.

The yarns used in the designs for this book are listed on page 11. All are made by Rowan Yarns and are available from all major stockists.

Wool Cotton is a merino wool and cotton mix. It is a soft yarn and has good stitch definition. It is machine washable.

All Seasons Cotton is a cotton and acrylic mix. It is a soft, yielding yarn that feels good and is a pleasure to work with.

Handknit Cotton is pure cotton and has a matt appearance. It is medium weight.

Cotton Rope is a cotton and acrylic mix. This is a heavy yarn, which is slightly thicker than Aran weight.

Cotton Glace is pure cotton. This yarn feels crisp as you work, and its surface has a slight shine.

Denim is pure cotton. It will shrink slightly and fade when washed, just like a pair of jeans.

4-ply Cotton is pure cotton. This has a more matt appearance than Cotton Glace and is slightly softer in texture.

Cashsoft Baby DK is a mix of extra-fine merino, microfibre and cashmere. This is a luxury yarn especially for babies.

Cashcotton 4-ply and **Cashcotton DK** are mixtures of cotton, polyamide, angora, viscose and cashmere. The yarns have a slightly hairy appearance but are soft to the touch.

Soft Baby is a mix of wool, polyamide and cotton. The yarn is soft, light and airy but reasonably bulky, which makes it fast to work with.

Cashsoft DK and **Cashsoft 4-ply** are mixtures of extra-fine merino, microfibre and cashmere. Available in two weights, these are very soft yarns.

4-ply Soft is pure merino. This delicate yarn is perfect for finely worked items.

crochet basics

Crochet is easy and quick to work, and you will need to be able to do just a few basic stitches to make the garments and accessories in this book.

Lace patterns and fancy shapes are achieved by simply combining some of the basic stitches, which are described below, and once you have mastered these few stitches you'll be able to make anything you like! Practise on a small square to start with, so you feel confident about holding a hook and so that the yarn slips easily through your fingers and from one stitch to another.

The first row of stitches worked into the chain should be worked under one thread of each stitch. In subsequent rows, unless otherwise specified, pass your hook under the top two horizontal threads of each stitch in the previous row.

The following diagrams show the hook held in the right hand. If you are left-handed, simply reverse the process. The diagrams are a mirror image of how you should proceed.

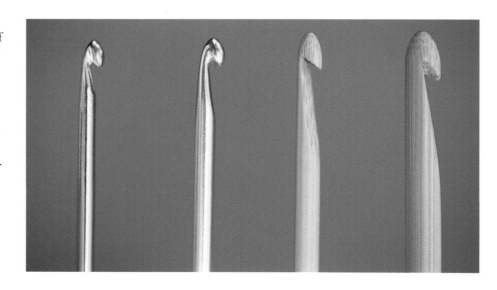

holding the hook

There is no definite rule about how you should hold a crochet hook. Two ways are shown here: in the first the hook is held as you would hold a pencil; in the second it is held as you would hold a knife. Choose whichever you feel comfortable with, but make sure that the hook faces downwards. You will find that your thumb automatically rests against the flat section found on most plastic and metal hooks.

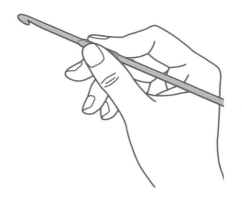

Hold the hook as you would a pencil.

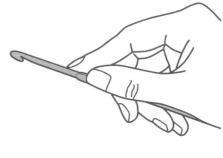

Alternatively you can hold the hook as you would a knife.

holding the yarn

The yarn is held in the left hand and is wound loosely around the fingers to maintain an even tension as you work.

To make a stitch use the first finger of your left hand to bring the yarn into position, from back to front, so that it can be caught by the hook and pulled through the loop on the hook to make a new loop.

As well as holding the yarn, the left hand holds the work.

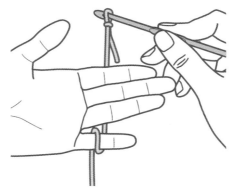

The yarn is wound loosely around the fingers of the left hand to maintain an even tension.

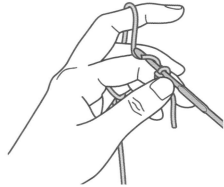

Use your left hand to hold your work as you crochet.

making a slip knot

Nearly all crochet begins with a slip knot, from which a chain is worked.

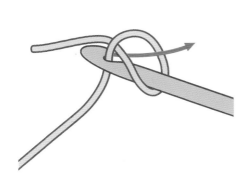

1 Make a loop as shown. Insert the hook through the loop and pull the yarn through the loop to make another loop.

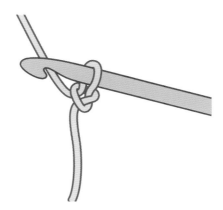

2 Tighten the loop by pulling gently on both ends of the yarn and slide the knot up to the hook.

chain stitch

The chain (ch) is the basis of all the patterns in this book. Count the stitches as you go along but do not count the slip knot as a stitch.

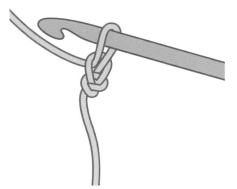

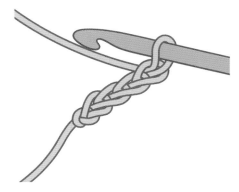

1 Start with a slip knot.

2 Wrap the yarn around the hook, from back to front, or catch it with the hook and pull the yarn through the loop already on the hook. This makes one chain stitch.

3 Repeat step 2 until you have the required length of chain. Remember, do not count the slip knot as a stitch.

slip stitch

Slip stitch (ss) involves pulling the yarn through 2 loops on the hook.

1 Make a chain and insert the hook into the second chain from the hook. Wrap the yarn around the hook by bringing it over the hook, from back to front. Pull the yarn through both loops on the hook. This makes one slip stitch.

2 Repeat step 1 into each stitch as required.

double crochet

Each double crochet (dc) makes 2 loops into the stitch on the previous row.

1 Make the required length of chain and insert the hook into the second chain from the hook. Wrap the yarn around the hook by bringing it over the hook from back to front. Pull the yarn through one loop only.

2 Wrap the yarn around the hook as in step 1 but this time pull it through both loops so that one loop is left on the hook. This makes one double crochet.

3 Repeat steps 1 and 2 into each chain to the end of the row or as required.

half treble

The half treble (htr) involves wrapping the yarn around the hook before you begin to make a stitch.

1 Wrap the yarn around the hook by bringing it over the hook from back to front. Insert the hook into the third chain from the hook. Do not pull the yarn through the loop.

2 Wrap the yarn around the hook as in step 1 and pull through one loop only to leave 3 loops on the hook.

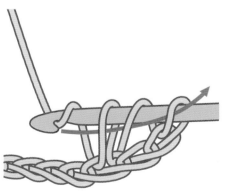

3 Wrap the yarn around the hook as in step 1 and pull through all 3 loops on the hook. This makes one half treble.

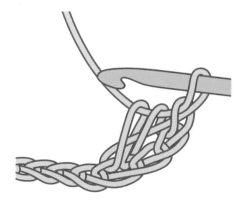

4 Repeat steps 1-3 in each chain to the end of the row or as required.

treble

The treble (tr) is used to create an open, rather lacy look.

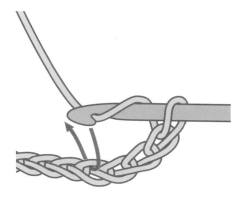

1 Wrap the yarn over the hook and insert the hook into the fourth chain from the hook. Wrap the yarn over the hook again and pull through 1 loop. There are now 3 loops on the hook.

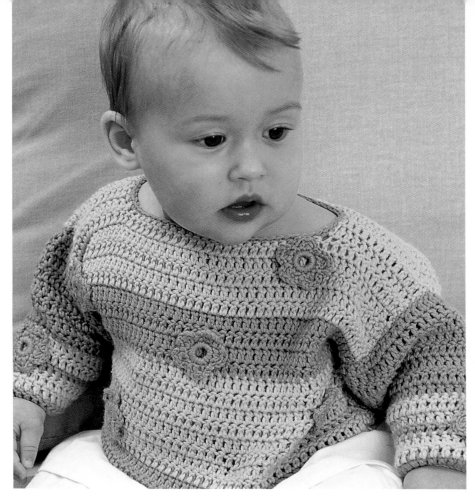

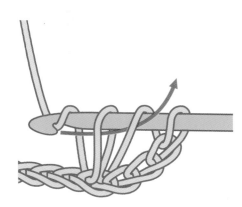

2 With 3 loops on the hook, wrap the yarn over the hook again. Bring the yarn through 2 loops only.

3 With 2 loops on the hook, wrap the yarn over the hook again. Bring the yarn through both loops on the hook so there is now one loop on the hook. This makes one treble.

4 Repeat steps 1-3 into each chain to the end of the row or as required.

turning the work on treble pattern

When the first row is complete you need to turn the work to do the next row. You can turn the work on either side but be consistent.

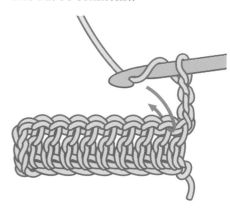

1 Work 3 chain stitches. These 3 stitches count as the first treble. Miss the last stitch of the previous row then work a treble into the next stitch.

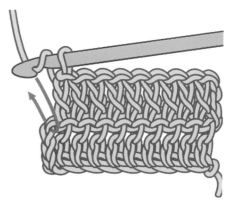

2 Work along the row by inserting the hook under the top 2 strands of each stitch in the previous row. At the end of the row work the last treble into the top of the 3 chain stitches from previous row.

working in rounds

When you are working in rounds, make sure that you keep the increases in the same position each time. Each round begins with a chain of a specified number of stitches, which counts as the first stitch.

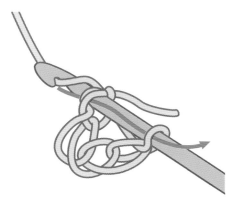

1 Work a chain as indicated in the pattern. Join the chain into a ring by making a slip stitch into the first chain.

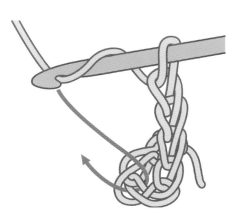

2 Make 3 chain stitches, which counts as the first treble. The first round is worked by inserting the hook into the centre of the chain ring.

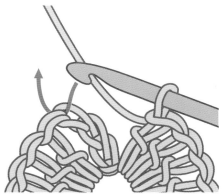

3 To join the round make a slip stitch into the top of the 3 chain made at the beginning of the round.

4 Continue working each round, starting with 3 chain stitches and working each treble under the top 2 strands of the stitch in the previous round unless otherwise stated.

finishing touches

Finishing your project well is essential for achieving a successful and professional-looking item. Although the processes involved can be time consuming, it will be time well spent, for careless finishing can spoil the effect of even the most beautiful crocheting.

neat edges

To make a neat, firm edge when changing colour work until 2 loops of the last stitch remain in the old colour, then use the new colour to complete the stitch.

yarn ends

The number of yarn ends left when an item is completed can be astonishing — and daunting. A quick way of tidying them is to weave a darning needle through the wrong side of the crochet and then thread the end through. This prevents short ends from slipping out of the needle as you weave them in.

joining seams

There are several methods of joining pieces of crochet together, and some use a tapestry needle, while others use a crochet hook. The seams may be decorative or invisible, depending on the work.

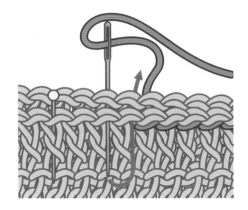

backstitch seam

This is a firm stitch, which does not stretch. Hold the work with right sides together. Match the stitches or row ends and use a tapestry needle to work backstitch as shown.

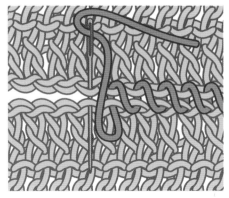

whip stitch

Whip stitch creates an invisible seam. Place the pieces edge to edge, wrong side up, and use a tapestry needle to work as shown.

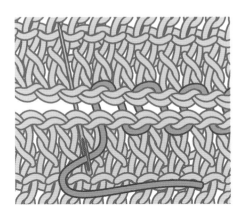

woven stitch

Use woven stitch when you want a flat, flexible seam. Place the pieces edge to edge, wrong sides up, and use a tapestry needle to stitch around the centre of each edge stitch as shown.

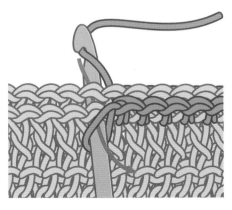

slip stitch

A slip stitch seam can be worked with wrong sides together so that the seam shows as a ridge on the right side of the work or with right sides together so that the seam is on the inside of the work. Insert a crochet hook through the corresponding stitches at each edge of the two pieces to be joined and work a slip stitch through each pair of stitches along the seam.

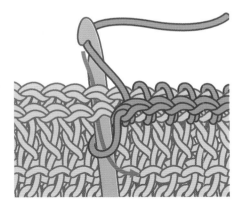

double crochet

As with a slip stitch seam, a double crochet seam can be worked with either the right sides or the wrong sides of the work facing. Work as for a slip stitch seam but use a double crochet stitch and work under two strands of each pair of stitches.

making a pompon

Cut two circles of card, each about 5 cm (2 in) across. Cut a small hole in the centre of each circle and make a single cut from the edge to the centre. Place the circles together, with the cuts opposite. Use a bodkin or blunt-ended tapestry needle to thread yarn round and round the circle, making sure that the yarn is evenly distributed around the central hole. Continue until the hole is full. Do not cut the long end of yarn yet. Use sharp-pointed scissors to snip the yarn between the two pieces of card, then wind the long end between the two card circles, fastening it as tightly as you can. Remove the card and trim the pompon to the required size, using the long end to attach the pompon to the garment as directed in the pattern.

making a decorative tassel

Take a piece of card about 10 cm (4 in) wide. Wind yarn around the card approximately 10 times then cut the yarn at one end. Fasten a short length of yarn around the centre of the threads to hold them together, then fold them together and bind another length of yarn about 2 cm (¾ in) down from the top. Tie firmly and trim the yarn to the required length.

making a basic tassel

Take a piece of card about 10 cm (4 in) wide. Wind yarn around the card about 10 times then cut the yarn at one end. Fold the lengths of yarn in half and thread the loop end through your work. Pass the loose ends through the loop end and pull tight to secure the tassel.

❋ out and about

baby mittens and bootees

Keep tiny toes and hands warm and cosy with these matching mittens and bootees, which would be the perfect gift for a newborn baby.

materials

Mittens

Striped: 1 50 g (1¼ oz) ball Rowan Cashcotton 4-ply in main shade (**MS**) Sugar 901 or Pretty 902; and 1 50 g (1¼ oz) ball in contrast (**C**) Cream 900

Solid: 1 50 g (1¼ oz) ball Rowan Cashcotton 4-ply in Cream 900 or Sugar 901 or Pretty 902

Bootees

Striped: 1 50 g (1¼ oz) ball Rowan Cashcotton 4-ply in main shade (**MS**) Cream 900; and 1 50 g (1¼ oz) ball in contrast (**C**) Sugar 901 or Pretty 902

Solid: 1 50 g (1¼ oz) ball Rowan Cashcotton 4-ply in Cream 900 or Sugar 901 or Pretty 902

2.50 mm (UK 12) crochet hook

sizes

Mittens

To fit 0-6 months;
length 9 cm (3½ in)

Bootees

To fit 0-3 months;
length of foot 9 cm (3½ in)

tension (gauge)

Mittens

26 sts and 30 rows to 10 cm (4 in) measured over double crochet worked with a 2.50 mm (UK 12) hook or the size required to achieve this tension.

Bootees

First 2 rounds measure 8 cm (3 in) long and 3 cm (1¼ in) wide worked with a 2.50 mm (UK 12) hook or the size required to achieve this tension.

abbreviations

beg beginning; **ch** chain; **cm** centimetre(s); **cont** continue; **dc** double crochet; **in** inch(es); **mm** millimetre(s); **patt** pattern; **rep** repeat; **RS** right side; **sp** space(s); **ss** slip stitch; **st(s)** stitch(es); **tr** treble; **tr12tog** (yoh and insert hook as indicated, yoh and draw loop through, yoh and draw through 2 loops) 12 times, yoh and draw through all 13 loops on hook; **yoh** yarn over hook

note

The instructions are for the striped mittens and bootees. For solid-colour mittens and bootees use one colour throughout but otherwise follow the pattern. The first chain in the pattern rows and rounds does not count as a stitch.

mittens (make 4)

With 2.50 mm (UK 12) hook and MS, make 7 ch.
Foundation row 1 dc into 2nd ch from hook, 1 dc into each ch to end, turn.
1st row (RS) 1 ch, 2 dc into first dc, 1 dc into each dc to last dc, 2 dc into last dc, turn. (8 sts)
Change to C.
2nd row 1 ch, 2 dc into first dc, 1 dc into each dc to last dc, 2 dc into last dc, turn. (10 sts)
3rd row As 2nd row. (12 sts)
Change to MS.
4th row As 2nd row. (14 sts)
5th row 1 ch, 1 dc into each dc to end, turn.
Change to C.
6th row As 5th row.
7th row As 5th row.
Cont working last row, keeping stripe patt correct for a further 12 rows.
Change to MS.
20th row 4 ch (counts as first tr, 1 ch), *1 tr into next dc, 1 ch, rep from * to last dc, 1 tr into last dc, turn.
21st row 4 ch (counts as first tr, 1 ch), *1 tr into next tr, 1 ch, rep from * to last tr, 1 tr into last tr, turn.
22nd row 1 ch, (1 dc, 3 ch, 1 dc) into first ch sp, *(1 dc, 3 ch, 1 dc) into next ch sp, rep from * to end.
Fasten off.

to finish

With RS together, sew around each mitten (see pages 20-21). Using MS work a chain about 30 cm (12 in) long and thread it through the last row of dc at the top of the mitten. Tie into a bow.

bootees (make 2)

With 2.50 mm (UK 12) hook and MS, make 15 ch.
1st round (RS) 3 tr into 3rd ch from hook, 1 tr into each of next 11 ch, 8 tr into last ch. Working back along the other side of foundation ch, work 1 tr into each of next 11 ch, 4 tr into same ch as first 3 tr of round, ss to top of 3 ch at beg of round. (38 sts)
2nd round 3 ch (counts as first tr), 1 tr into st at base of 3 ch, 1 tr into next tr, 2 tr into next tr, 1 tr into each of next 13 tr, 2 tr into next tr, 1 tr into next tr, 2 tr into each of next 2 tr, 1 tr into next tr, 2 tr into next tr, 1 tr into each of next 13 tr, 2 tr into next tr, 1 tr into next tr, 2 tr into next tr, ss to top of 3 ch at beg of round. (46 sts)
3rd round 1 ch, 1 dc into first st, 2 dc into next tr, 1 dc into each of next 19 tr, 2 dc into next tr, 1 dc into each of next 2 tr, 2 dc into next tr, 1 dc into each of next 19 tr, 2 dc into next tr, 1 dc into last tr, ss to back loop of first dc. (50 sts)
Join in C.
4th round Using C, 1 ch, working into back loops only of previous round, 1 dc into each dc to end, ss to first dc.
5th round Using MS, 1 ch, 1 dc into each dc to end, ss to first dc.
6th round Using C, 1 ch, 1 dc into each dc to end, ss to first dc.
7th round As 5th round.
Do not fasten off but set MS to one side.

shape top of foot

With 2.50 mm (UK 12) hook and separate length of C, miss first 12 sts of next round, join yarn to next st and cont as follows.
1st row (RS) 3 ch (counts as first tr), (miss 1 dc, 1 tr into next dc) 12 times, turn. (13 sts)
2nd row 1 ch, 1 dc into each tr to end, working last dc into top of 3 ch at beg of previous row, turn. (13 sts)
3rd row 3 ch, tr12tog over next 12 dc, 1 ch, fasten off.

shape ankle

Pick up MS and, with RS facing, work into top of 7th round and row-end edges of top of foot as follows.

8th round 5 ch (counts as first tr, 2 ch), miss dc at base of 5 ch and next dc, 1 tr into next dc, 2 ch, miss 1 dc, 1 tr into next dc, (2 ch, miss 2 dc, 1 tr into next dc) twice, 2 ch, miss 1 dc, 1 tr into next dc (this is same dc where yarn was joined for top of foot), 2 ch, 1 tr into row-end edge of 2nd row of top of foot, 2 ch, 1 tr into fasten-off point of top of foot, 2 ch, 1 tr into other row-end edge of 2nd row of top of foot, 2 ch, miss 1 dc, (1 tr into next dc, 2 ch, miss 2 dc) twice, (1 tr into next dc, 2 ch, miss 1 dc) 3 times, ss to 3rd of 5 ch at beg of round. (14 ch sp)

9th round Using C, ss into first ch sp, 3 ch (counts as first tr), 1 tr into same ch sp, 1 ch, miss 1 tr, *2 tr into next ch sp, 1 ch, miss 1 tr, rep from * to end, ss to top of 3 ch at beg of round.

10th round Using MS, ss across and into first ch sp, 1 ch, 2 dc into same ch sp, miss 2 tr, *2 dc into next ch sp, miss 2 tr, rep from * to end, ss to first dc. (28 sts)

11th round Using C, 1 ch, 1 dc into each dc to end, ss to first dc.

12th round Using MS, 1 ch, 1 dc into each dc to end, ss to first dc.

13th round As 11th round.

14th round Using MS, 1 ch, (1 dc, 3 ch and 1 dc) into first dc, miss 1 dc, *(1 dc, 3 ch and 1 dc) into next dc, miss 1 dc, rep from * to end, ss to first dc. Fasten off.

sole seam trim

Fold bootee along 4th round and, with RS of sole facing and 2.50 mm (UK 12) hook, join MS to one front loop of 3rd round at heel and cont as follows: 1 ch, 1 dc into each front loop of sts of 3rd round, ending with ss to first dc.
Fasten off.

to finish

Use MS to make 2 crochet or twisted cords, each about 33 cm (13 in) long, and thread them through the holes of 8th round. Tie the ends in a bow at the front of each bootee.

lacy hat and scarf

This matching hat and scarf set is made in a very pretty shell stitch. The hat is gathered at the top, so no shaping is required.

materials

Hat
2 (2; 3) 50 g (1¼ oz) balls Rowan Wool Cotton in Flower 943
Scarf
1 50 g (1¼ oz) ball Rowan Wool Cotton in Flower 943
3.50 mm (UK 9) crochet hook

sizes

Hat
To fit ages 6-12 months (1-2; 2-3 years)
Scarf
10 x 86 cm (4 x 34 in)

tension (gauge)

25 sts and 12 rows to 10 cm (4 in) measured over lace patt worked with a 3.50 mm (UK 9) hook or the size required to achieve this tension.

abbreviations

beg beginning; **ch** chain; **cm** centimetre(s); **cont** continue; **dc** double crochet; **in** inch(es); **mm** millimetre(s); **patt** pattern; **rep** repeat; **ss** slip stitch; **st(s)** stitch(es); **tr** treble

hat (worked in one piece)

With 3.50 mm (UK 9) hook, make 96 (104; 112) ch, ss into first ch to form a ring.

1st round 1 ch, *miss 3 ch, 1 tr in next ch, (1 ch, 1 tr) 4 times in same ch as tr just made, miss 3 ch, 1 dc in next ch, rep from * to end.

2nd round 6 ch, miss first dc, *miss (1 tr, 1 ch) twice, 1 dc in next tr (the centre tr of 5), 3 ch, miss (1 ch, 1 tr) twice, 1 tr in dc, 3 ch, rep from *, ending with 3 ch, ss into 3rd of 6 ch at beg of round.

3rd round 1 ch, miss first tr, *miss 3 ch, 1 tr in dc, (1 ch, 1 tr) 4 times in same dc as tr just made, miss 3 ch, 1 dc in tr, rep from *, ending with ss into first ch at beg of round.

Rounds 2 and 3 form the patt. Cont in patt until work measures 22 (23.5; 25) cm (8½; 9¼; 10 in), ending with 3rd round of patt.

Fasten off.

to finish

Work a chain about 25 cm (10 in) long. Make 2 small pompons (see page 23). Thread the chain through the patt of the hat 5 patt rows down from the top. Attach a pompon to each end of the chain and tie a knot to pull in the top of the hat. Sew in any loose ends.

scarf

With 3.50 mm (UK 9) hook, make 25 ch.

Foundation row Miss first 4 ch, * 1 tr into next ch, (1 ch, 1 tr) 4 times in same ch as tr just made, miss 3 ch, 1 dc into next ch, miss 3 ch, rep from *, ending with 1 dc into last ch, turn.

1st row 6 ch, miss first dc, * miss (1 tr, 1 ch) twice, 1 dc into next tr (the centre tr of 5), 3 ch, miss (1 ch, 1 tr) twice, 1 tr in next dc, 3 ch, rep from *, ending with 1 tr in ch after last tr, turn.

2nd row 1 ch, miss first tr, * miss 3 ch, 1 tr in dc, (1 ch, 1 tr) 4 times in same dc as tr just made, miss 3 ch, 1 dc in tr, rep from *, ending 1 dc in 3rd of 6 ch, turn.

Rows 1 and 2 form the patt. Cont in patt until the work measures 86 cm (34 in), ending with 1st row of patt.

to finish

With a 3.50 mm (UK 9) hook and starting at one corner of the scarf, work 1 row of dc evenly around edge of scarf. Fasten off. Sew in any loose ends.

perfect poncho

Worked in bright stripes and finished with pompon ties, this is the ideal way to keep warm on days out and trips to the beach.

materials

2 (2; 3) 50 g (1¾ oz) balls Rowan Cashcotton DK in main shade (**MS**) Apple 603; 2 (2; 3) 50 g (1¾ oz) balls Rowan Cashcotton DK in 1st contrast (**1st C**) Pool 602; and 2 (2; 3) 50 g (1¾ oz) balls Rowan Cashcotton DK in 2nd contrast (**2nd C**) White 600
4.00 mm (UK 8) crochet hook

sizes

To fit

1-2	2-3	3-4	years

To fit chest

51	56	61	cm
20	22	24	in

Actual size at hem

153	169	186	cm
60¼	66½	73¼	in

Centre back length

32	36	40	cm
12½	14	15¾	in

tension (gauge)

17 sts and 15 rows to 10 cm (4 in) measured over half treble st worked with a 4.00 mm (UK 8) hook or the size required to achieve this tension.

abbreviations

beg beginning; **ch** chain; **cm** centimetre(s); **cont** continue; **dc** double crochet; **dec** decreas(e)(es)(ing); **patt** pattern; **htr** half treble; **htr2tog** (yoh and insert hook as indicated, yoh and draw loop through) twice, yoh and draw through all 5 loops on hook; **htr3tog** (yoh and insert hook as indicated, yoh and draw loop through) 3 times, yoh and draw through all 7 loops on hook; **in** inch(es); **mm** millimetre(s); **patt** pattern; **rem** remaining; **rep** repeat; **RS** right side; **ss** slip stitch; **st(s)** stitch(es); **tr** treble; **yoh** yarn over hook

2 ch, 1 htr into each of next 60 (67; 74) htr, (htr3tog over next 3 sts) twice, 1 htr into each of next 60 (67; 74) htr, 1 htr into top of 2 ch at beg of previous row, turn. (124; 138; 152 sts)

2nd row 2 ch (counts as first htr), miss htr at base of 2 ch, 1 htr into each of next 59 (66; 73) htr, (htr2tog over next 2 sts) twice, 1 htr into each of next 59 (66; 73) htr, 1 htr into top of 2 ch at beg of previous row, turn. (122; 136; 150 sts)

3rd row 2 ch (counts as first htr), miss htr at base of 2 ch, 1 htr into each of next 57 (64; 71) htr, (htr3tog over next 3 sts) twice, 1 htr into each of next 57 (64; 71) htr, 1 htr into top of 2 ch at beg of previous row, turn. (118; 132; 146 sts)

Join in 1st C.

4th row Using 1st C, 2 ch (counts as first htr), miss htr at base of 2 ch, 1 htr into each of next 56 (63; 70) htr, (htr2tog over next 2 sts) twice, 1 htr into each of next 56 (63; 70) htr, 1 htr into top of 2 ch at beg of previous row, turn. (116; 130; 144 sts)

5th row Using 1st C, 2 ch (counts as first htr), miss htr at base of 2 ch, 1 htr into each of next 54 (61; 68) htr, (htr3tog over next 3 sts) twice, 1 htr into each of next 54 (61; 68) htr, 1 htr into top of 2 ch at beg of previous row, turn. (112; 126; 140 sts)

6th row Using 1st C, 2 ch (counts as first htr), miss htr at base of 2 ch, 1 htr into each of next 53 (60; 67) htr, (htr2tog over next 2 sts) twice, 1 htr into each of next 53 (60; 67) htr, 1 htr into top of 2 ch at beg of previous row, turn. (110; 124; 138 sts)

7th row Using 1st C, 2 ch (counts as first htr), miss htr at base of 2 ch, 1 htr into each of next 51 (58; 65) htr, (htr3tog over next 3 sts) twice, 1 htr into each of next 51 (58; 65) htr, 1 htr into top of 2 ch at beg of previous row, turn. (106; 120; 134 sts)

Join in 2nd C.

8th row Using 2nd C, 2 ch (counts as first htr), miss htr at base of 2 ch, 1 htr into each of next 50 (57; 64) htr, (htr2tog over next 2 sts) twice, 1 htr into each of next 50 (57; 64) htr, 1 htr into top of 2 ch at beg of previous row, turn. (104; 118; 132 sts)

9th row Using 2nd C, 2 ch (counts as first htr), miss htr at base of 2 ch, 1 htr into each of next 48 (55; 62) htr, (htr3tog over next 3 sts) twice, 1 htr into each of next 48 (55; 62) htr, 1 htr into top of 2 ch at beg of

back

With 4.00 mm (UK 8) hook and MS, make 131 (145; 159) ch.

Foundation row (RS) 1 htr into 3rd ch from hook, 1 htr into each of next 61 (68; 75) ch, (htr2tog over next 2 ch) twice, 1 htr into each of rem 63 (70; 77) ch, turn. (128; 142; 156 sts)

Cont in patt as follows.

1st row 2 ch (counts as first htr), miss htr at base of

previous row, turn. (100; 114; 128 sts)

10th row Using 2nd C, 2 ch (counts as first htr), miss htr at base of 2 ch, 1 htr into each of next 47 (54; 61) htr, (htr2tog over next 2 sts) twice, 1 htr into each of next 47 (54; 61) htr, 1 htr into top of 2 ch at beg of previous row, turn. (98; 112; 126 sts)

11th row Using 2nd C, 2 ch (counts as first htr), miss htr at base of 2 ch, 1 htr into each of next 45 (52; 59) htr, (htr3tog over next 3 sts) twice, 1 htr into each of next 45 (52; 59) htr, 1 htr into top of 2 ch at beg of previous row, turn. (94; 108; 122 sts)

Last 12 rows form stripe sequence (4 rows in each colour) and set centre shaping (3 sts dec at each side of centre on every 2 rows – 6 sts in total dec on every 2 rows).*

Cont as set, keeping stripes and dec correct, as follows.

Work a further 20 (24; 28) rows, ending after 4 rows using 1st C (2nd C; MS) and a WS row. (34; 36; 38 sts)

Fasten off.

front

Work as for Back to *.

Cont as set, keeping stripes and dec correct, as follows.

Work a further 12 (16; 20) rows, ending after 4 rows using 2nd C (MS; 1st C) and a WS row. (58; 60; 62 sts)

Divide for front opening

Keeping stripes correct, cont as follows.

Next row (RS) 2 ch (counts as first htr), miss htr at base of 2 ch, 1 htr into each of next 26 (27; 28) htr, htr2tog over next 2 sts and turn, leaving rem 29 (30; 31) sts unworked.

Work on this set of sts only for first side.

Next row 2 ch (does not count as st), miss st at base of 2 ch, htr2tog over next 2 sts, 1 htr into each st to end, working last htr into top of 2 ch at beg of previous row, turn.

Next row 2 ch (counts as first htr), miss htr at base of 2 ch, 1 htr into each htr to last 2 sts, htr2tog over last 2 sts, turn.

Rep last 2 rows twice more, then first of these rows again. (17; 18; 19 sts)

Fasten off.

Return to last complete row worked, rejoin

appropriate yarn to next st and cont as follows.

Next row (RS) 2 ch (does not count as st), miss htr where yarn was rejoined, 1 htr into each htr to end, working last htr into top of 2 ch at beg of previous row, turn.

Next row 2 ch (counts as first htr), miss htr at base of 2 ch, 1 htr into each htr to last 3 sts, htr3tog over last 3 sts, turn.

Next row 2 ch (does not count as st), miss st at base of 2 ch, 1 htr into each htr to end, working last htr into top of 2 ch at beg of previous row, turn.

Rep last 2 rows twice more, then first of these rows again. (17; 18; 19 sts)

Fasten off.

to finish

Join side and overarm seams (see pages 20-21).

hem edging

With RS facing and using 4.00 mm (UK 8) hook, attach MS to base of one side seam, 1 ch (does not count as st), *1 dc into base of side seam, work 62 (68; 74) dc across foundation ch edge to base of point, 1 dc between the 2 htr2tog of foundation row, 62 (68; 74) dc across foundation ch edge to next side seam, rep from * once more, ss to first dc. (252; 276; 300 sts)

Next round 1 ch (does not count as st), 1 dc into first dc, *miss 2 dc, 6 tr into next dc, miss 2 dc, 1 dc into next dc, rep from * to end, replacing dc at end of last rep with ss to first dc.

Fasten off.

neck edging and ties

With RS facing and using 4.00 mm (UK 8) hook, attach 1st C (2nd C; MS) to top of left side of front neck opening, 1 ch (does not count as st), work 1 row of dc evenly down first side of opening, then up second side of opening, 26 ch, 1 dc into 2nd ch from hook, 1 dc into each of next 24 ch (for first tie), work 1 dc into each st around neck edge, 26 ch, 1 dc into 2nd ch from hook, 1 dc into each of next 24 ch (for second tie), ss to dc at beg of round.

Fasten off.

Make 2 small pompons (see page 23) using all 3 colours and attach them to the ends of the ties.

denim backpack

Made with denim yarn, this bag will fade like a favourite pair of jeans. Adjustable straps allow the backpack to 'grow' with your child.

materials

3 50 g (1¼ oz) balls Rowan Denim in main shade (**MS**) Memphis 229; 2 50 g (1¼ oz) balls Rowan Denim in 1st contrast (**1st C**) Tennessee 231; and 2 50 g (1¼ oz) balls Rowan Denim in 2nd contrast (**2nd C**) Ecru 324
4.00 mm (UK 8) crochet hook
3.50 mm (UK 9) crochet hook
4 small buttons
2 small beads

size

26 x 26 cm (10 x 10 in)

tension (gauge)

15 sts and 9 rows to 10 cm (4 in) measured over treble crochet worked with a 4.00 mm (UK 8) hook before washing or the size required to achieve this tension. Each square on the front measures 6 x 6 cm (2½ in) before washing.

abbreviations

beg beginning; **ch** chain; **cont** continue; **dc** double crochet; **mm** millimetre(s); **rep** repeat; **RS** right side; **ss** slip stitch; **st(s)** stitch(es); **cm** centimetre(s); **in** inch(es); **tr** treble(s); **WS** wrong side

back

With 4.00 mm (UK 8) hook and MS, make 48 ch.
1st row (RS) 1 tr into 4th ch from hook, 1 tr into each ch to end, turn.
2nd row 3 ch (counts as first tr), miss first tr, 1 tr into each tr to end, turn.
Rep 2nd row, changing colours as follows.
Work 1 row in 2nd C.
Work 3 rows in 1st C.
Work 1 row in MS.
Work 2 rows in 2nd C.
Work 1 row in 1st C.
Work 1 row in 2nd C.
Work 2 rows in MS.
Work 3 rows in 2nd C.
Work 1 row in MS.
Work 4 rows in 1st C.
Work 1 row in MS.
Work 2 rows in 2nd C.
Work 1 row in 1st C.
Fasten off.

front
for one square

With 4.00 mm (UK 8) hook and MS, make 4 ch, join with ss to form a ring.
1st round 5 ch (counts as 1 tr, 2 ch), (3 tr into ring, 2 ch) 3 times, 2 tr into ring, ss into 3rd of 5 ch at beg of round.
2nd round ss into next ch, 7 ch (counts as 1 tr, 4 ch) *2 tr into same arch, 1 tr into each tr across side of square**, 2 tr into next arch, 4 ch, rep from * twice and from * to ** again, 1 tr into same arch as 7 ch, ss into 3rd of 7 ch at beg of round.
Fasten off.
Make a further 8 squares in MS.
Make 8 squares in 1st C.
Make 8 squares in 2nd C.

straps (make 2)

With 4.00 mm (UK 8) hook and MS, make 80 ch.
1st row 1 tr into 4th ch from hook, 1 tr into each ch to end, turn.
Change to 1st C.
2nd row 1 ch (counts as first dc), miss first st, 1 dc

into each st to end, turn.
Change to 2nd C.
3rd row Work as 2nd row.
Change to MS.
4th row 3 ch (counts as first tr), miss first dc, 1 tr
into each dc to end.
Fasten off.

tie

With 4.00 mm (UK 8) hook and 1st C, make 130 ch.
Fasten off.

to finish

Wash all pieces of work and long lengths of each
colour according to the instructions on the ball band.

front

Sew in any loose ends.
Lay out the squares, using the photograph as a guide to
the colour sequence.
With 3.50 mm (UK 9) hook and a length of 1st C that
has been washed, put 2 squares that will be adjacent
with WS together and join by inserting the hook
through corresponding sts of each edge and working a
dc through each pair of sts along the seam, working up
the bag (see pages 20-21). Do not break the yarn. Cont

to join in 2 squares as you work up the bag until the
row is complete. Join the next row of squares to the
row just worked and cont until all squares have been
joined on the front.
With RS of front and back facing, put 1 end of each
strap into seam at each corner of bag across bottom.
Join down both side seams and across bottom.
Attach the 4 buttons on the back at centre top,
positioning the first 2 buttons 3 rows down, side
by side and strap width apart. Position the second
2 buttons about 4 cm (1½ in) down from the top 2
buttons. This is to attach the straps so that you can
adjust the length.
Weave the tie evenly through the top of bag, beg at
centre front. Attach beads to the ends of the tie. Sew
in any loose ends.

tassel hat

Cute tassels are a great finishing touch to this soft and cosy hat. Try different colour combinations to match your child's favourite winter coat.

materials

1 (1; 2) 50 g (1¼ oz) balls Rowan Wool Cotton in main shade (**MS**) Elf 946; 1 (1; 2) 50 g (1¼ oz) balls Rowan Wool Cotton in 1st contrast (**1st C**) Citron 901; and 1 (1; 2) 50 g (1¼ oz) balls Rowan Wool Cotton in 2nd contrast (**2nd C**) Mellow Yellow 942
4.00 mm (UK 8) crochet hook

sizes

To fit ages 6-12 months (1-2; 3-4 years)

tension (gauge)

18 sts and 11 rows to 10 cm (4 in) measured over patt worked with a 4.00 mm (UK 8) hook or the size required to achieve this tension.

abbreviations

ch chain; **cm** centimetre(s); **dc** double crochet; **in** inch(es); **mm** millimetre(s); **patt** pattern; **rep** repeat; **RS** right side; **st(s)** stitch(es); **tr** treble

hat (worked in one piece)

With 4.00 mm (UK 8) hook and MS, make 79 (85; 91) ch.

Foundation row (RS) 5 tr into 4th ch from hook, *miss 2 ch, 1 dc into next ch, miss 2 ch, 5 tr into next ch, rep from * to last ch, 1 dc into last ch, turn.
Change to 1st C.

1st row 3 ch, 2 tr into first dc, *miss 2 tr, 1 dc into next tr (the centre of 5 tr), miss 2 tr, 5 tr into next dc, rep from *, ending 3 tr into 1 ch, turn.
Change to 2nd C.

2nd row 1 ch, miss first 3 tr, *5 tr into next dc, miss 2 tr, 1 dc into next tr (the centre of 5 tr), miss 2 tr, rep from *, ending 1 dc into 3rd of 3 ch from previous round, turn.

These 3 rows form the stripe patt.

Rep rows 1 and 2 for patt throughout, changing colour every row using all 3 colours until hat measures 16 (17, 18) cm (6¼; 6½; 7 in). Fasten off.

to finish

Sew the back seam (see pages 20–21). Sew across the top of the hat, making sure the seam goes to the back of the head.
Make 2 big basic tassels (see page 23) using all 3 colours and attach them to each corner of hat.
Sew in any loose ends.

diamond scarf

Liven up dull winter days with this brightly patterned scarf. The soft 4-ply yarn is perfect against delicate skin. Work wider bands of colour for a bolder effect.

materials

2 50 g (1¾ oz) balls Rowan 4-ply soft in main shade (**MS**) Nippy 376; 1 50 g (1¾ oz) ball Rowan 4-ply soft in 1st contrast (**1st C**) Wink 377; 1 50 g (1¾ oz) ball Rowan 4-ply soft in 2nd contrast (**2nd C**) Splash 373; and 1 50 g (1¾ oz) ball Rowan 4-ply soft in 3rd contrast (**3rd C**) Buzz 375 3.00 mm (UK 11) crochet hook

size

13 x 108 cm (5 x 42½ in)

tension (gauge)

32 sts and 13 rows to 10 cm (4 in) measured over diamond patt worked with a 3.00 mm (UK 11) hook or the size required to achieve this tension.

abbreviations

ch chain; **cm** centimetre(s); **cont** continue; **dc** double crochet; **in** inch(es); **mm** millimetre(s); **patt** pattern; **rep** repeat; **RS** right side; **st(s)** stitch(es); **tr** treble

note

To make a neat edging when you are changing colour see page 20.

scarf

With 3.00 mm (UK 11) hook and MS, make 50 ch.
1st row (RS) Miss 3 ch (counts as first tr), 2 tr into next ch, *miss 3 ch, 1 dc into next ch, 3 ch, 1 tr into each of next 3 ch, rep from * to last 4 ch, miss 3 ch, 1 dc into last ch, turn.
Change to 1st C.
2nd row 3 ch (counts as first tr), 2 tr into first dc, *miss 3 tr, 1 dc into first of 3 ch, 3 ch, 1 tr into each of next 2 ch, 1 tr into next dc, rep from *, ending miss 2 tr, 1 dc into top of 3 ch at beg of previous row, turn.
Rep row 2 throughout, changing colour every row for stripe patt as follows.
Change to MS, work 1 row.
Change to 2nd C, work 1 row.
Change to MS, work 1 row.
Change to 3rd C, work 1 row.
Change to MS, work 1 row.
Cont working in stripe patt until work measures 108 cm (42½ in).
Fasten off.

to finish

With 3.00 mm (UK 11) hook and MS, work 1 row of dc evenly down both sides of the scarf. Make basic tassels (see page 23) and attach to each end of the scarf at each point of the patt. Sew in any loose ends.

flower bag

This cheerful bag is quick and easy to make, and the flower detail makes it a pretty addition to any little girl's wardrobe.

materials

1 50 g (1¾ oz) ball Rowan Handknit DK Cotton in main shade **(MS)** Rosso 215; 1 50 g (1¾ oz) ball Rowan Handknit DK Cotton in 1st contrast **(1st C)** Slick 313; and 1 50 g (1¾ oz) ball Rowan Handknit DK Cotton in 2nd contrast **(2nd C)** Gooseberry 219
5.00 mm (UK 6) crochet hook
3.50 mm (UK 9) crochet hook

size

12 x 12 cm (4¾ x 4¾ in)

tension (gauge)

13 sts and 15 rows to 10 cm (4 in) measured over double crochet worked with a 5.00 mm (UK 6) hook using 2 ends of yarn or the size required to achieve this tension.

abbreviations

ch chain; **cm** centimetre(s); **cont** continue; **dc** double crochet; **in** inch(es); **mm** millimetre(s); **rep** repeat; **RS** right side; **ss** slip stitch; **st(s)** stitch(es)

bag (make 2)

With 5.00 mm (UK 6) hook and using 1 end of MS and 1 end of 1st C together, make 16 ch.

Foundation row (RS) 1 dc into 2nd ch from hook, 1 dc into each ch to end, turn. (15 sts)

1st row 1 ch (counts as first dc), miss first dc, 1 dc into each dc, turn.

2nd row 1 ch (counts as first dc), miss first dc, 1 dc into each dc, ending 1 dc into 1ch, turn.

Cont working 2nd row until work measures 12 cm (4¾ in). Fasten off.

strap

With 5.00 mm (UK 6) hook and 1 end of MS and 1 end of 1st C together, make 92 ch.

Work 1 row of dc. Fasten off.

large flower

With 3.50 mm (UK 9) hook and 2nd C, make 6 ch, join with a ss to form a ring.

1st round 1 dc into ring, *20 ch, 1 dc into ring, rep from * 12 more times. Fasten off.

medium flower

With 3.50 mm (UK 9) hook and MS, make 6 ch, join with a ss to form a ring.

1st round 1 dc into ring, *14 ch, 1 dc into ring, rep from * 12 more times.
Fasten off.

small flower

With 3.50 mm (UK 9) hook and 1st C, make 6 ch, join with a ss to form a ring.

1st round 1 dc into ring, *8 ch, 1 dc into ring, rep from * 12 more times.
Fasten off.

to finish

Sew front and back together down both side seams and across bottom (see pages 20-21). Sew the large flower in the centre of one side. Sew the medium flower in the centre of the large flower and the small flower in the centre of the medium flower. Sew the strap to the inside of each side of the bag. Sew in any loose ends.

✱ fun to wear

waistcoat

This versatile waistcoat can be worn over a T-shirt or with a shirt for special occasions. Choose buttons to match the contrast edgings.

materials

3 (4; 4) 50 g (1¾ oz) balls Rowan Cashsoft DK in main shade (**MS**) Poppy 512; and 1 (1; 1) 50 g (1¾ oz) ball in contrast (**C**) Navy 514
4.00 mm (UK 8) crochet hook
4 buttons

sizes

To fit ages

1-2	2-3	3-4	years

To fit chest

56	59	61	cm
22	23	24	in

Actual size

57	62	68	cm
22½	24½	26¼	in

Length

33	36	38	cm
13	14	15	in

tension (gauge)

21 sts and 15 rows to 10 cm (4 in) measured over patt worked with a 4.00 mm (UK 8) hook or the size required to achieve this tension.

abbreviations

ch chain; **cm** centimetre(s); **cont** continue; **dc** double crochet; **in** inch(es); **mm** millimetre(s); **patt** pattern; **rep** repeat; **RS** right side; **sp** space(s); **ss** slip stitch; **st(s)** stitch(es); **tr** treble; **WS** wrong side

back

With 4.00 mm (UK 8) hook and MS, make 61 (65; 69) ch.

Foundation row (RS) (1 tr, 1 ch, 1 tr) in 3rd ch from hook, *miss 1 ch, 1 dc into next ch, miss 1 ch, (1 tr, 1 ch, 1 tr) in next ch, rep from * to last 2 ch, miss 1 ch, 1 dc in last ch, turn. (61; 65; 69 sts)

1st row 4 ch, miss (first dc and 1 tr), *1 dc into 1 ch sp, 1 ch, miss 1 tr, 1 tr into next dc, 1 ch, miss 1 tr, rep from *, ending 1 dc in last ch sp, 1 ch, miss 1 tr, 1 tr in next tr, turn.

2nd row 1 ch, miss first tr, *miss 1 ch, (1 tr, 1 ch, 1 tr) in next dc, miss 1 ch, 1 dc in next tr, rep from *, working last dc into 3rd of 4 ch, turn.

Rep 1st and 2nd rows until work measures 19 (20; 21) cm (7½; 8; 8¼ in), ending after a 1st row.

shape armholes

Next row ss across 9 sts and in same 9th st work 1 ch, miss 1 tr, *miss 1 ch, (1 tr, 1 ch, 1 tr) into next dc, miss 1 ch, 1 dc into next tr, rep from * to last 8 sts, turn. (45; 49; 53 sts)

Cont in patt, starting with 1st row, until work measures 33 (36; 38) cm (13; 14; 15 in), ending after a 1st row.

Fasten off.

left front

With 4.00 mm (UK 8) hook and MS, make 29 (33; 37) ch.

Work in patt as for back until work measures 19 (20; 21) cm (7½; 8; 8¼ in), ending after a 1st row.

shape armhole

Next row ss across 9 sts and in same 9th st work 1 ch, miss 1 tr, *miss 1 ch, (1 tr, 1 ch, 1 tr) into next dc, miss 1 ch, 1 dc in next tr, rep from *, working last dc into 3rd of 4th ch, turn.

Cont in patt until work measures 33 (36; 38) cm (13; 14; 15 in), ending after a 1st row.

Fasten off.

right front

Work in patt as for left front to armhole shaping.

shape armhole

Next row 1 ch, miss first tr, *miss 1 ch, (1 tr, 1 ch, 1 tr) in next dc, miss 1 ch, 1 dc in next tr, rep from

* to last 8 sts, turn.

Cont in patt until work measures 33 (36, 38) cm (13; 14; 15 in), ending after a 1st row.

Fasten off.

to finish

Mark shoulder seams 5 (5.5; 6) cm (2; 2¼; 2½ in) in from armholes. Sew side and shoulder seams (see pages 20-21). With 4.00 mm (UK 8) hook and C, starting at side seam, work 1 row of dc evenly around all edges. Work 1 row of dc around armhole edges. Fold back collar to start of shoulder seam and 12 (14; 16) cm (4¾; 5½; 6¼ in) down from shoulder and hold in place with a few sts on WS. Sew 4 buttons evenly spaced down left front, using patt on other side for buttonholes. Sew in loose ends.

ribbon-tie suntop

This pretty suntop has ribbons for shoulder straps, which look adorable tied in matching bows, and the back is fastened with tiny buttons.

materials

2 (2) 50 g (1¼ oz) balls Rowan 4-ply Cotton in main shade (**MS**) Tutti Frutti 138; and 1 (1) 50 g (1¼ oz) ball Rowan Cotton Glace in contrast (**C**) Ecru 725
3.00 mm (UK 11) crochet hook
9-10 buttons
4 lengths of ribbon, each about 38 cm (15 in)

sizes

To fit ages

2-3	3-4	years

To fit chest

56	61	cm
22	24	in

Actual size (excluding trim)

52	57	cm
20½	22½	in

Full length (excluding trim)

22	25	cm
8½	10	in

tension (gauge)

24 sts and 15 rows to 10 cm (4 in) measured over patt worked with a 3.00 mm (UK 11) hook or the size required to achieve this tension.

abbreviations

ch chain; **cm** centimetre(s); **cont** continue; **dc** double crochet; **in** inch(es); **mm** millimetre(s); **patt** pattern; **rep** repeat; **RS** right side; **ss** slip stitch; **st(s)** stitch(es); **tr** treble

suntop (worked in one piece)

With 3.00 mm (UK 11) hook and MS, make 126 (138) ch.

Foundation row 1 dc into 6th ch from hook, *2 ch, miss 2 ch, 1 dc into next ch, rep from * to end, turn.

1st row (RS) 3 ch, 1 tr into first dc, *miss 2 ch, 3 tr into next dc, rep from *, ending miss 2 ch, 2 tr into next ch, turn.

Change to C.

2nd row 1 ch, miss first tr, *2 ch, miss 2 tr, 1 dc into next tr, (centre tr of 3), rep from *, ending 1 dc into 3rd of 3 ch, turn.

Change to MS.

Rep rows 1 and 2 until work measures 22 (25) cm (8½; 10 in), ending with a 1st row.

to finish

With 3.00 mm (UK 11) hook and C, rejoin yarn to bottom right corner of suntop. Work 1 row of dc evenly around all the sides of the suntop, making sure that all sides are divisible by 6 for the scallop edging.

Next row 1 ch, *miss 2 dc, 6tr into next dc, miss 2 dc, 1 dc into next dc, rep from * all the way around the 4 sides, working 3 dc into each corner. Fasten off. Fold the 2 sides into the centre to form the back seam. Sew buttons on to each scallop along the edge of the right back, using the scallops on the other side for buttonholes.

Sew the lengths of ribbon to the inside of the suntop, about 3 scallops in from the sides.

flower (make 2)

With 3.00 mm (UK 11) hook and MS, make 5 ch, ss into first ch to form a ring.

Next round 1 ch, (1 dc into ring, 8 ch) 9 times, 1 dc into ring.

Fasten off.

Sew in any loose ends. Attach flowers to the front at the base of the ribbon ties.

flower sweater

This cute and snuggly sweater is a great addition to any child's wardrobe. Don't add the flower decorations if you're making it for a boy.

materials

2 (2; 2) 50 g (1¾ oz) balls Rowan Wool Cotton in main shade (**MS**) Aqua 949; 1 (1; 1) 50 g (1¾ oz) ball Rowan Wool Cotton in 1st contrast (**1st C**) Clear 941; and 1 (1; 1) 50 g (1¾ oz) ball Rowan Wool Cotton in 2nd contrast (**2nd C**) Mellow Yellow 942

4.00 mm (UK 8) crochet hook

3.50 mm (UK 9) crochet hook

1 button

sizes

To fit ages			
6–12 mths	1–2	2–3	years
To fit chest			
46	51	56	cm
18	20	22	in
Actual size			
53	59	65	cm
20¾	23¼	25½	in
Full length			
24	26	30	cm
9½	10¼	11¾	in
Sleeve seam			
14	18	24	cm
5½	7	9½	in

tension (gauge)

19 sts and 10 rows to 10 cm (4 in) measured over treble crochet worked with a 4.00 mm (UK 8) hook or the size required to achieve this tension.

abbreviations

alt alternate; **beg** beginning; **ch** chain; **cm** centimetre(s); **cont** continue; **dc** double crochet; **in** inch(es); **inc** increas(e)(ing); **mm** millimetre(s); **patt** pattern; **rem** remain(ing); **RS** right side; **ss** slip stitch; **st(s)** stitch(es); **tr** treble; **tr2tog** work 1 tr into each of next 2 dc until 1 loop of each remains on hook, yoh and draw through all 3 loops on hook; **WS** wrong side; **yoh** yarn over hook

Return to last complete row worked, miss centre 2 tr, rejoin appropriate yarn to next tr and cont as follows.
Next row 3 ch (counts as first tr), miss tr where yarn was rejoined, 1 tr into each tr to end, working last tr into top of 3 ch at beg of previous row, turn.
Work a further 5 rows on these 24 (27; 30) sts, ending after 4 (2; 2) rows using 2nd C (MS; 1st C) and after a RS row.
Fasten off.

front
Work as for Back to **.
Cont in striped tr patt for a further 9 (11; 15) rows, ending after a WS row.
Shape neck
Next row (RS) 3 ch (counts as first tr), miss tr at end of previous row, 1 tr into each of next 12 (14; 16) tr and turn, leaving rem sts unworked.
Work a further 2 rows on these 13 (15; 17) sts, ending after 4 (2; 2) rows using 2nd C (MS; 1st C) and after a RS row.
Fasten off.
Return to last complete row worked, miss centre 24 (26; 28) tr, rejoin appropriate yarn to next tr and cont as follows.
Next row 3 ch (counts as first tr), miss tr where yarn was rejoined, 1 tr into each tr to end, working last tr into top of 3 ch at beg of previous row, turn.
Work a further 2 rows on these 13 (15; 17) sts, ending after 4 (2; 2) rows using 2nd C (MS; 1st C) and after a RS row.
Fasten off.

sleeve (make 2)
With 4.00 mm (UK 8) hook and MS, make 27 (29; 31) ch.
Foundation row (WS) 1 tr into 4th ch from hook, 1 tr into each ch to end, turn. (25; 27; 29 sts)
Cont in tr patt, shaping sides as follows.
Join in 1st C.
1st row Using 1st C, 3 ch (counts as first tr), miss tr at end of previous row, 2 tr into next tr (1 st inc), 1 tr into each tr to last 2 sts, 2 tr into next tr (1 st inc), 1 tr into top of 3 ch at beg of previous row, turn.
This row forms tr patt and starts sleeve shaping.

back
With 4.00 mm (UK 8) hook and MS, make 52 (58; 64) ch.
Foundation row (WS) 1 tr into 4th ch from hook, 1 tr into each ch to end, turn. (50; 56; 62 sts)
Cont in tr patt as follows.
1st row 3 ch (counts as first tr), miss tr at end of previous row, 1 tr into each tr to end, working last tr into top of 3 ch at beg of previous row, turn.
This row forms tr patt. Cont in tr patt in stripes as follows.
Using MS, work a further 2 rows.
Join in 1st C and work 4 rows.
Join in 2nd C and work 4 rows.
Last 12 rows form stripe sequence.**
Cont in striped tr patt for a further 6 (8; 12) rows, ending after a RS row.
Divide for back opening
Next row (WS) 3 ch (counts as first tr), miss tr at end of previous row, 1 tr into each of next 23 (26; 29) tr, turn, leaving rem sts unworked.
Work a further 5 rows on these 24 (27; 30) sts, ending after 4 (2; 2) rows using 2nd C (MS; 1st C) and after a RS row.
Fasten off.

Cont in tr patt in stripes as follows.

Join in 2nd C and work 1 row, inc 1 st at each end of row. (29; 31; 33 sts)

Last 3 rows form stripe sequence.

Cont in striped tr patt, shaping sides by inc 1 st at each end of next 3 (3; 4) rows, then on 0 (0; 1) following alt row. (35; 37; 43 sts)

Break off 1st C and 2nd C and cont in tr patt with MS only.

Inc 1 st at each end of next (next; 2nd) and following 6 (4; 0) rows, then on following 0 (3; 6) alt rows. (49; 53; 57 sts)

Work 1 row, ending after a RS row.

Fasten off.

neck border

Join shoulder seams.

With RS facing and using 4.00 mm (UK 8) hook, rejoin MS to base of back opening, 1 ch (does not count as st), work 1 row of dc evenly around entire neck and back opening edge, working 2 dc into corners at top of back opening. Fasten off.

Sew ends of Neck Border in place at base of back opening.

to finish

Mark points along side seam edges 13 (14; 15) cm (5; 5½; 6 in) either side of shoulder seams and sew Sleeves to Back and Front between these points. Join side and sleeve seams (see pages 20-21).

Make a button loop and attach button to fasten top of back neck opening.

flower (make 14)

With 3.50 mm (UK 9) hook and MS, make 6 ch, ss into first ch to form a ring.

1st round 1 ch, work 15 dc into ring, ss into first dc.

2nd round (3 ch, tr2tog over next 2 dc, 3 ch, ss into next dc) 5 times, placing last ss into last dc of previous round.

Fasten off.

Sew 6 flowers on the front, 6 on the back and 1 on each sleeve of the girl's sweater (using the photograph as a guide).

Breton-style sweater

Made with cotton yarn, this sweater is ideal for chilly summer evenings. Make it in bright colours for a girl's version.

materials

5 50 g (1¾ oz) balls Rowan Handknit DK Cotton in main shade (**MS**) Turkish Plum 277; and 4 50 g (1¾ oz) balls Rowan Handknit DK Cotton in contrast (**C**) Linen 205
4.00 mm (UK 8) crochet hook
3 buttons

sizes

To fit ages

2-3	3-4	years

To fit chest

56	61	cm
22	24	in

Actual size

60	70	cm
23½	27½	in

Full length

34	38	cm
13¼	15	in

Sleeve seam

25	29	cm
10	11½	in

tension (gauge)

15 sts and 9 rows to 10 cm (4 in) measured over treble crochet worked on a 4.00 mm (UK 8) hook or the size required to achieve this tension.

abbreviations

beg beginning; **ch** chain; **cm** centimetre(s); **cont** continue; **dc** double crochet; **in** inch(es); **inc** increas(e)(ing); **mm** millimetre(s); **patt** pattern; **rep** repeat; **RS** right side; **ss** slip stitch; **st(s)** stitch(es); **tr** treble; **WS** wrong side

back

With 4.00 mm (UK 8) hook and MS, make 47 (55) ch.
Foundation row (WS) 1 tr into 4th ch from hook, 1 tr into each ch to end, turn. (45; 53 sts)
Cont in tr patt as follows.
1st row 3 ch (counts as first tr), 1 tr into each tr to end, working last tr into top of 3 ch at beg of previous row, turn.
This row forms tr patt.
Cont in tr patt in stripes as follows.
Work 2 rows in C.
Work 2 rows in MS.
Cont in stripe patt until work measures 18 (21) cm (7; 8¼ in).

shape armholes

Next row ss over first 4 sts, and in same 4th st work 3 ch (counts as first tr), 1 tr into each tr to last 3 sts, turn, leaving last 3 sts unworked. (39; 47sts)
Cont in stripe patt until work measures 34 (38) cm (13¼; 15 in), ending after a full 2-row stripe.
Fasten off.

front

Work as for Back until work measures 31 (35) cm (12¼; 13¾ in) (3 rows down from top).

shape front neck

Next row 3 ch (counts as first tr), 1 tr into each of next 11 (14) tr, turn.
Next row ss over first 2 tr and into same 2nd st work 3 ch (counts as first tr), 1 tr into each tr to end, turn.
Next row 3 ch (counts as first tr), 1 tr into each of next 9 (12) tr.
Fasten off.
Leaving centre 15 (17) sts unworked, rejoin yarn to last 12 (15) sts.
Next row 3 ch (counts as first tr), 1 tr into each tr to end, turn.
Next row 3 ch (counts as first tr), 1 tr into each of next 10 (13) tr, turn.
Next row ss over first 2 tr and into same 2nd st work 3 ch (counts as first tr), 1 tr into each tr to end.
Fasten off.

sleeve (make 2)

With 4.00 mm (UK 8) hook and MS, make 24 (26) ch.
Foundation row (WS) 1 tr into 4th ch from hook, 1 tr into each ch to end, turn. (22; 24 sts)
Next row (inc row) 3 ch (counts as first tr), 2 tr into next tr, 1 tr into each tr to last 2 tr, 2 tr into next tr, 1 tr into top of 3 ch, turn. (24; 26 sts)
Cont in stripe patt as back and inc as follows.
Rep the last row 5 times more. (34; 36 sts)
Next row 3 ch (counts as first tr), 1 tr into each tr to end, turn.
Next row (inc row) 3 ch (counts as first tr), 2 tr into next tr, 1 tr into each tr to last 2 tr, 2 tr into next tr, 1 tr into top of 3 ch, turn.
Rep the last 2 rows, inc on every alt row, until there are 48 (50) sts.
Cont straight until sleeve measures 25 (29) cm (10; 11½ in), finishing with a full stripe rep.
Work a further 2 rows in stripe patt.
Fasten off.

to finish

Sew side and sleeve seams (see pages 20-21).

Shoulder fastening

With 4.00 mm (UK 8) hook, MS and WS facing, rejoin yarn to back left shoulder 9 (12) sts.
Next row 3 ch (counts as first tr), 1 tr into each of next 9 (12) tr, turn.
Next row 3 ch (counts as first tr), 1 tr into each tr to end.
Fasten off.
Sew right shoulder seam. Sew 3 buttons evenly along left front shoulder
Sew sleeves into armholes.
With 4.00 mm (UK 8) hook and MS and starting at front left shoulder, work 1 row of dc along shoulder, around front neck, along back neck and around shoulder fastening. Fasten off. Sew in any loose ends.

boy's or girl's cardigan

A cropped princess-style cardigan with beads and sequins is perfect with a party dress, while a longer version with chunky buttons looks great on little boys.

materials

Cropped cardigan
3 (4; 4) 50 g (1¾ oz) balls Rowan Cashsoft DK in Bella Donna 502
Long cardigan
5 (6; 6) 50 g (1¾ oz) balls Rowan Cashsoft DK in Ballad Blue 508
4.00 mm (UK 8) crochet hook
5 buttons (cropped cardigan)
8 buttons (long cardigan)
Beads and sequins (cropped cardigan)

sizes

To fit ages

1-2	2-3	3-4	years

To fit chest

51	56	61	cm
20	22	24	in

Actual size

58	64	71	cm
22¾	25	28	in

Cropped cardigan full length

18	19	21	cm
7	7½	8¼	in

Long cardigan full length

33	36	41	cm
13	14	16	in

Sleeve seam

21	29	33	cm
8¼	11½	13	in

tension (gauge)

18 sts and 12 rows to 10 cm (4 in) measured over patt worked with a 4.00 mm (UK 8) hook or the size required to achieve this tension.

abbreviations

beg beginning; **ch** chain; **cm** centimetre(s); **cont** continue; **dc** double crochet; **in** inch(es); **mm** millimetre(s); **patt** pattern; **rem** remain(ing); **rep** repeat; **RS** right side; **sp** space(s); **ss** slip stitch; **st(s)** stitch(es); **tr** treble; **WS** wrong side

back

With 4.00 mm (UK 8) hook, make 53 (59; 65) ch.

Foundation row (WS) 1 dc into 2nd ch from hook, *2 ch, miss 2 ch, 1 dc into next ch, rep from * to end, turn. (52; 58; 64 sts)

Cont in patt as follows.

1st row (RS) 3 ch (counts as first tr), 1 tr into dc at base of 3 ch, *miss 2 ch, 3 tr into next dc, rep from * to last 3 sts, miss 2 ch, 2 tr into last dc, turn.

2nd row 1 ch (does not count as st), 1 dc into first tr, *2 ch, miss 2 tr, 1 dc into next tr, rep from * to end, working last dc into top of 3 ch at beg of previous row, turn.

These 2 rows form patt.

cropped cardigan
Work in patt for 1 row more, ending after a RS row.

long cardigan
Work in patt for a further 19 (21; 25) rows, ending after a RS row.

shape armholes (both cardigans)
Next row (WS) ss across and into 7th st, 1 ch (does not count as st), 1 dc into same tr as last ss, *2 ch, miss 2 tr, 1 dc into next tr, rep from * to last 6 sts and turn, leaving rem 6 sts unworked. (40; 46; 52 sts)

Work a further 15 (17; 19) rows without shaping, ending after a RS row.

Fasten off, placing markers either side of centre 22 (24; 26) sts to denote back neck.

left front

With 4.00 mm (UK 8) hook, make 29 (32; 35) ch.

Work foundation row as for Back. (28; 31; 34 sts)

cropped cardigan
Work in patt as for Back for 3 rows, ending after a RS row.

long cardigan
Work in patt as for Back for 21 (23; 27) rows, ending after a RS row.

shape armhole (both cardigans)
Next row (WS) 1 ch (does not count as st), 1 dc into first tr, *2 ch, miss 2 tr, 1 dc into next tr, rep from * to last 6 sts and turn, leaving rem 6 sts unworked. (22; 25; 28 sts)

Work a further 10 (12; 14) rows without shaping, ending after a WS row.

shape neck (both cardigans)
Next row (RS) 3 ch (counts as first tr), 1 tr into dc at base of 3 ch, (miss 2 ch, 3 tr into next dc) 3 (4; 5) times, miss 2 ch, 1 tr into next dc and turn, leaving rem 9 sts unworked.

Next row ss across and into 3rd st, 1 ch (does not count as st), 1 dc into same tr as last ss, *2 ch, miss 2 tr, 1 dc into next tr, rep from * to end, working last dc into top of 3 ch at beg of previous row, turn.

Next row 3 ch (counts as first tr), 1 tr into dc at base of 3 ch, (miss 2 ch, 3 tr into next dc) 2 (3; 4) times, miss 2 ch, 1 tr into next dc, turn.

Next row 1 ch (does not count as st), 1 dc into first tr, 1 ch, miss 1 tr, 1 dc into next tr, *2 ch, miss 2 tr, 1 dc into next tr, rep from * to end, working last dc into top of 3 ch at beg of previous row, turn.

Next row 3 ch (counts as first tr), 1 tr into dc at base of 3 ch, (miss 2 ch, 3 tr into next dc) 2 (2; 3) times, miss 1 (2; 2) ch, 1 (2; 2) tr into next dc, (1 tr into next ch sp) 0 (1; 0) times.

Fasten off rem 9 (11; 13) sts.

right front

With 4.00 mm (UK 8) hook, make 29 (32; 35) ch.
Work foundation row as for Back. (28; 31; 34 sts)

cropped cardigan

Work in patt as for Back for 3 rows. End after a RS row.

long cardigan

Work in patt as for Back for 21 (23; 27) rows, ending
after a RS row.

shape armhole (both cardigans)

Next row (WS) ss across and into 7th st, 1 ch (does not
count as st), 1 dc into same tr as last ss, *2 ch, miss 2 tr,
1 dc into next tr, rep from * to end, working last dc into
top of 3 ch at beg of previous row, turn. (22; 25; 28 sts)
Work a further 10 (12; 14) rows without shaping,
ending after a WS row.

shape neck (both cardigans)

Next row (RS) ss across and into 10th st, 3 ch (does
not count as st), (miss 2 ch, 3 tr into next dc) 3 (4; 5)
times, miss 2 ch, 2 tr into last dc, turn.
Next row 1 ch (does not count as st), 1 dc into first tr,
(2 ch, miss 2 tr, 1 dc into next tr) 3 (4; 5) times, turn.
Next row 3 ch (counts as first tr), miss 1 dc and 2 ch,
(3 tr into next dc, miss 2 ch) 2 (3; 4) times, miss 2 ch,
2 tr into last dc, turn.
Next row 1 ch (does not count as st), 1 dc into first
tr, (2 ch, miss 2 tr, 1 dc into next tr) 2 (3; 4) times,
1 ch, miss 1 tr, 1 dc into top of 3 ch at beg of previous
row, turn.
Next row (ss into first ch sp) 0 (1; 0) times, (ss across
and into 3rd st) 0 (0; 1) times, 3 ch (counts as first tr),
(2 tr into next dc) 0 (1; 0) times, (1 tr into dc at base
of 3 ch) 0 (0; 1) times, miss 1 (2; 2) ch, (3 tr into next
dc, miss 2 ch) 2 (2; 3) times, 2 tr into last dc.
Fasten off rem 9 (11; 13) sts.

sleeve (make 2)

With 4.00 mm (UK 8) hook, make 26 (32; 38) ch.
Work foundation row as for Back. (25; 31; 37 sts)
Work in patt as for Back for 1 (1; 3) rows, ending after
a RS row.

shape sleeve

1st row (WS) As 2nd patt row.
2nd row 3 ch (counts as first tr), 2 tr into dc at base
of 3 ch, *miss 2 ch, 3 tr into next dc, rep from * to
end, turn.

3rd row 1 ch (does not count as st), 1 dc into each of first 2 tr, *2 ch, miss 2 tr, 1 dc into next tr, rep from * to last st, 1 dc into top of 3 ch at beg of previous row, turn.

4th row 3 ch (counts as first tr), miss st at base of 3 ch, 3 tr into next dc, *miss 2 ch, 3 tr into next dc, rep from * to last st, 1 tr into last dc, turn.

5th row 1 ch (does not count as st), 1 dc into first tr, 2 ch, miss 1 tr, 1 dc into next tr, *2 ch, miss 2 tr, 1 dc into next tr, rep from * to last 2 sts, 2 ch, miss 1 tr, 1 dc into top of 3 ch at beg of previous row, turn.

6th row 3 ch (counts as first tr), 1 tr into st at base of 3 ch, *miss 2 ch, 3 tr into next dc, rep from * to last 3 sts, miss 2 ch, 2 tr into last dc, turn. (31; 37; 43 sts)
Work 0 (2; 2) rows.
Rep last 6 (8; 8) rows 3 times more. (49; 55; 61 sts)
Work a further 0 (0; 2) rows, ending after a RS row.
Place markers at both ends of top of last row.
Work a further 4 rows, ending after a RS row.
Fasten off.

to finish

Join shoulder seams (see pages 20-21). Matching sleeve markers to top of side seam and centre of last row of sleeves to shoulder seam, sew sleeves into armholes. Join side and sleeve seams.

front opening, hem and neck edging

With RS facing and using 4.00 mm (UK 8) hook, rejoin yarn to base of one side seam, 1 ch (does not count as st), work 1 round of dc evenly across hem edge, up right front opening edge, around neck, down left front opening edge, and across rem section of hem edge, working 3 dc into corner points and ending with ss to first dc. (For Cropped Cardigan make sure that the number of dc worked is divisible by 6.)

cropped cardigan only

Next round 1 ch (does not count as st), 1 dc into first dc, *miss 2 dc, 6 tr into next dc, miss 2 dc, 1 dc into next dc, rep from * to end, replacing dc at end of last rep with ss to first dc.

both cardigans

Fasten off.

cuff edgings (both cardigans)

Work as for Front Opening, Hem and Neck Edging.

long cardigan

Attach buttons about 4 sts in from inner edge of edging of appropriate front opening edge, spacing buttons evenly along edge and using spaces between trs on other front as buttonholes.

cropped cardigan

Attach buttons to left side of cardigan on the centre of each shell edging. Use the shell edge on the other side as buttonholes.

Attaching each sequin with a bead, sew 3 sequins on each shell of edging around neck, cuffs and lower edge.

happy hoodie

This hoodie is suitable for a girl or a boy and the stripes make it really striking. For a special touch you could try adding fancy buttons.

materials

2 (2; 3; 3) 50 g (1¾ oz) balls Rowan Cashsoft DK in main shade (**MS**) Poppy 512; 2 (2; 3; 3) 50 g (1¾ oz) balls Rowan Cashsoft DK in contrast (**C**) Cream 500
4.00 mm (UK 8) crochet hook
5 buttons

sizes

To fit age

0-6	6-12 mths	1-2	2-3	years

To fit chest

41	46	51	56	cm
16	18	20	22	in

Actual size

42	48	54	61	cm
16½	18¾	21¼	24	in

Full length

22	25	29	33	cm
8¼	9¾	11½	13	in

Sleeve seam

13	14.5	20	24	cm
5	5¼	7¼	9½	in

tension (gauge)

19 sts and 22 rows to 10 cm (4 in) measured over double crochet worked with a 4.00 mm (UK 8) hook or the size required to achieve this tension.

abbreviations

ch chain; **cm** centimetre(s); **cont** continue; **dc** double crochet; **dc2tog** (insert hook as indicated, yoh and draw loop through) twice, yoh and draw through all 3 loops on hook; **dec** decreas(e)(es) (ing); **in** inch(es); **inc** increas(e)(ing); **mm** millimetre(s); **patt** pattern; **rem** remain(ing); **rep** repeat; **RS** right side; **sp** space(s); **ss** slip stitch; **st(s)** stitch(es); **WS** wrong side; **yoh** yarn over hook

back

With 4.00 mm (UK 8) hook and MS, make 40 (46; 52; 58) ch.

Foundation row (RS) 1 dc into 2nd ch from hook, 1 dc into each ch to end, turn. (39; 45; 51; 57 sts)
Cont in dc patt as follows.

1st row 1 ch (does not count as st), 1 dc into each dc to end, turn.
This row forms dc patt.
Cont in dc patt in stripes as follows.
Join in C and work 2 rows.
Using MS, work 2 rows.
Last 4 rows form stripe sequence.
Cont in striped dc patt for a further 20 (26; 32; 38) rows, ending after 2 rows using MS (C; MS; C) and a WS row.

shape armholes

Next row (RS) ss across and into 3rd st, 1 ch (does not count as st), 1 dc into same dc as used for last ss and each dc to last 2 dc, turn, leaving rem 2 sts unworked. (35; 41; 47; 53 sts)

Next row 1 ch (does not count as st), dc2tog over first 2 sts, 1 dc into each dc to last 2 sts, dc2tog over last 2 sts, turn.
Rep last row twice more. (29; 35; 41; 47 sts)
Work a further 18 (20; 22; 24) rows without shaping, ending after 2 rows using C and a WS row.
Fasten off, marking centre 17 (19; 21; 23) sts to denote back neck.

left front

With 4.00 mm (UK 8) hook and MS, make 23 (26; 29; 32) ch.
Work foundation row as for Back. (22; 25; 28; 31 sts)

for a girl

Cont in striped dc patt as for Back for 25 (31; 37; 43) rows, ending after 2 rows using MS (C; MS; C) and a WS row.

for a boy

Cont in striped dc patt as for Back for 7 rows, ending after 2 rows using C and a WS row.

Next row (RS) 1 ch (does not count as st), 1 dc into each dc to last 4 dc, 2 ch (to make a buttonhole: on following row, work 2 dc into this ch sp), miss 2 dc, 1 dc into each of last 2 dc, turn.
Making a further 4 buttonholes in this way on every following 6th (8th; 10th; 12th) row and noting that no further reference will be made to buttonholes, cont as follows.
Cont in striped dc patt for a further 17 (23; 29; 35) rows, ending after 2 rows using MS (C; MS; C) and a WS row.

shape armhole (both garments)

Next row (RS) ss across and into 3rd st, 1 ch (does not count as st), 1 dc into same dc as used for last ss and each dc to end, turn. (20; 23; 26; 29 sts)
Working all armhole dec in same way as for Back, dec 1 st at armhole edge of next 3 rows. (17; 20; 23; 26 sts)
Work a further 18 (20; 22; 24) rows without shaping, ending after 2 rows using C and after a WS row.
Fasten off, placing a marker after 6th (8th; 10th; 12th) st in from armhole edge to denote neck shoulder point.

right front

With 4.00 mm (UK 8) hook and MS, make 23 (26; 29; 32) ch.

Work foundation row as for Back. (22; 25; 28; 31 sts)

for a girl

Cont in striped dc patt as for Back for 7 rows, ending after 2 rows using C and a WS row.

Next row (RS) 1 ch (does not count as st), 1 dc into each of first 2 sts, 2 ch (to make a buttonhole: on following row, work 2 dc into this ch sp), miss 2 dc, 1 dc into each dc to end, turn.

Making a further 4 buttonholes in this way on every following 6th (8th; 10th; 12th) row and noting that no further reference will be made to buttonholes, cont as follows.

Cont in striped dc patt for a further 17 (23; 29; 35) rows, ending after 2 rows, using MS (C; MS; C) and a WS row.

for a boy

Cont in striped dc patt as for Back for 25 (31; 37; 43) rows, ending after 2 rows using MS (C; MS; C) and a WS row.

shape armhole (both garments)

Next row (RS) 1 ch (does not count as st), 1 dc into each dc to last 2 dc, turn, leaving rem 2 sts unworked. (20; 23; 26; 29 sts)

Working all armhole dec in same way as for Back, dec 1 st at armhole edge of next 3 rows. (17; 20; 23; 26 sts)

Work a further 18 (20; 22; 24) rows without shaping, ending after 2 rows using C and after a WS row.

Fasten off, placing a marker after 6th (8th; 10th; 12th) st in from armhole edge to denote neck shoulder point.

sleeve (make 2)

With 4.00 mm (UK 8) hook and MS, make 24 (26; 28; 30) ch.

Work foundation row as for Back. (23; 25; 27; 29 sts)

Cont in striped dc patt as for Back for 2 rows, ending after 1 row using C and a RS row.

Next row 1 ch (does not count as st), 2 dc into first dc (1 st inc), 1 dc into each dc to last st, 2 dc into last dc (1 st inc), turn.

This row sets sleeve shaping.

Cont in striped dc patt, shaping sides by inc 1 st at each end of every following 2nd (2nd; 3rd; 3rd) row to 33 (33; 37; 35) sts, then on every foll 3rd (3rd; 4th; 4th) row until there are 41 (45; 49; 53) sts.

Work a further 4 (4; 4; 6) rows without shaping,

ending after 2 rows using C and a WS row.

shape top

Next row (RS) ss across and into 3rd st, 1 ch (does not count as st), 1 dc into same dc as used for last ss and each dc to last 2 dc, turn, leaving rem 2 sts unworked. (37; 35; 39; 43) sts.

Next row 1 ch (does not count as st), dc2tog over first 2 sts, 1 dc into each dc to last 2 sts, dc2tog over last 2 sts, turn.

Rep last row twice more. (31; 35; 39; 43) sts.

Fasten off.

hood

Join shoulder seams.

With RS facing and using 4.00 mm (UK 8) hook, rejoin MS to top of right front opening edge, 1 ch (does not count as st), work 1 dc into each of the 11 (12; 13; 14) dc across right front neck edge, work across back neck 17 (19; 21; 23) dc as follows: 2 dc into next dc, (1 dc into next dc, 2 dc into next dc) 8 (9; 10; 11) times, then work 1 dc into each of the 11 (12; 13; 14) dc across left front neck edge, turn. (48; 53; 58; 63 sts)

Work in striped dc patt for a further 36 (40; 44; 48) rows, ending after 1 row using MS and a RS row.

Fold Hood in half with RS facing and work 1 row of dc through both layers to close top seam.

Fasten off.

to finish

Join side and sleeve seams (see pages 20-21). Insert sleeves.

front opening and hood edging

With RS facing and using 4.00 mm (UK 8) hook, rejoin MS to base of right front opening edge, 1 ch (does not count as st), work 1 row of dc evenly up right front opening edge, around hood and down left front opening edge, turn.

Now work a further row of dc around edge.

Fasten off.

Make a small pompon in MS (see page 23) and attach it to the point on the hood. Attach buttons to correspond with buttonholes.

bath robe

Wrap up warm after a bath in this gorgeous robe. Try making the two-tone edging in colours to match a favourite pair of pyjamas.

materials

9 (10; 11) 50 g (1¾ oz) balls Rowan All Seasons Cotton in main shade (**MS**) Bleached 182; 1 (1; 1) 50 g (1¾ oz) ball Rowan All Seasons Cotton in 1st contrast (**1st C**) Lime Leaf 217; and 1 (1; 1) 50 g (1¾ oz) ball Rowan All Seasons Cotton in 2nd contrast (**2nd C**) Giddy 203
5.00 mm (UK 6) crochet hook

sizes

To fit age

1-2	2-3	3-4	years

To fit chest

51	56	61	cm
20	22	24	in

Actual size

62	68	74	cm
24½	26¾	29	in

Full length

52	60	65	cm
20½	23½	25½	in

Sleeve seam

20	22	27	cm
8	8¾	10½	in

tension (gauge)

13 sts and 7 rows to 10 cm (4 in) measured over patt worked with a 5.00 mm (UK 6) hook or the size required to achieve this tension.

abbreviations

beg beginning; **ch** chain; **cm** centimetre(s); **cont** continue; **dc** double crochet; **in** inch(es); **inc** increas(e)(ing); **mm** millimetre(s); **patt** pattern; **rep** repeat; **RS** right side; **ss** slip stitch; **st(s)** stitch(es); **tr** treble; **WS** wrong side

back

With 5.00 mm (UK 6) hook and MS, make 42 (46; 50) ch.

Foundation row (RS) 2 tr into 4th ch from hook, *miss 1 ch, 2 tr into next ch, rep from * to last 2 ch, miss 1 ch, 1 tr into last ch, turn. (40; 44; 48 sts)
Cont in patt as follows.

1st row 3 ch (counts as first tr), miss tr at base of 3 ch, *2 tr into next tr, miss 1 tr, rep from * to last st, 1 tr into top of 3 ch at beg of previous row, turn.
This row forms patt.
Cont in patt for a further 38 (44; 48) rows, ending after a WS row.
Fasten off, placing markers either side of centre 16 (20; 24) sts to denote back neck.

left front

With 5.00 mm (UK 6) hook and MS, make 26 (30; 34) ch.
Work foundation row as for Back. (24; 28; 32 sts)
Work in patt as for Back for 39 (45; 49) rows, ending after a WS row.
Fasten off.

right front

Work as for Left Front.

sleeve (make 2)

With 5.00 mm (UK 6) hook and MS, make 22 (24; 26) ch.
Work foundation row as for Back. (20; 22; 24 sts)
Work in patt as for Back for 1 row, ending after a WS row.

shape sleeve

1st row (RS) 3 ch (counts as first tr), 1 tr into base of 3 ch (1 st inc), *2 tr into next tr, miss 1 tr, rep from * to last st, 2 tr into top of 3 ch at beg of previous row (1 st inc), turn.
2nd row 3 ch (counts as first tr), 1 tr into base of 3 ch (1 st inc), 1 tr into next tr, *2 tr into next tr, miss 1 tr, rep from * to last 2 sts, 1 tr into next tr, 2 tr into top of 3 ch at beg of previous row (1 st inc), turn.
Rep last 2 rows 1 (1; 0) times more. (28; 30; 28 sts)
Next row (RS) 3 ch (counts as first tr), 1 tr into base of 3 ch (1 st inc), *2 tr into next tr, miss 1 tr, rep from * to last st, 2 tr into top of 3 ch at beg of previous row (1 st inc), turn.
Next row 3 ch (counts as first tr), miss tr at base of 3 ch, 1 tr into next tr, *2 tr into next tr, miss 1 tr, rep from * to last 2 sts, 1 tr into next tr, 1 tr into top of 3 ch at beg of previous row, turn.
Next row 3 ch (counts as first tr), 1 tr into base of 3 ch (1 st inc), 1 tr into next tr, *2 tr into next tr, miss 1 tr, rep from * to last 2 sts, 1 tr into next tr, 2 tr into top of 3 ch at beg of previous row (1 st inc), turn.
Next row 3 ch (counts as first tr), miss tr at base of 3 ch, *2 tr into next tr, miss 1 tr, rep from * to last st, 1 tr into top of 3 ch at beg of previous row, turn. (32; 34; 32 sts)
Rep last 4 rows 1 (1; 3) times more, then first 0 (2; 0) of these rows again. (36; 40; 44 sts)
Fasten off.

hood

Join shoulder seams (see pages 20-21).
With RS facing and using 5.00 mm (UK 6) hook, rejoin MS to top of right front opening edge and work across right front neck 12 (16; 20) sts as follows: 3 ch (counts as first tr), miss tr at base of 3 ch, (2 tr into

next tr, miss 1 tr) 5 (7; 9) times, 2 tr into last tr, then work across back neck 16 (20; 24) sts as follows: (2 tr into first tr) 1 (0; 0) times, (2 tr into next tr, miss 1 tr, 2 tr into next tr) 5 (6; 8) times, (2 tr into next tr, miss last tr) 0 (1; 0) times, then work across left front neck 12 (16; 20) sts as follows: 2 tr into first tr, (2 tr into next tr, miss 1 tr) 5 (7; 9) times, 1 tr into top of 3 ch at beg of last row of left front, turn. (48; 60; 74 sts)
Work in patt as for Back for 15 (17; 17) rows, ending after a WS row.
Fold Hood in half with RS facing and work 1 row of dc through both layers to close top seam.
Fasten off.

to finish

Mark points along side seam edges 14 (16; 17) cm (5½; 6¼; 6¾ in) either side of shoulder seams and sew sleeves to back and fronts between these points. Join side and sleeve seams.

front opening, hem and hood edging

With RS facing and using 5.00 mm (UK 6) hook, attach 1st C to base of one side seam, 1 ch (does not count as st), work 1 round of dc evenly around entire hem, front opening and hood edges, working 3 dc into hem corner points and ending with ss to first dc.
Next round 1 ch (does not count as st), 1 dc into each dc to end, working 3 dc into hem corner points and ending with ss to first dc.
Break off 1st C and join in 2nd C.
Rep last round once more.
Fasten off.

cuff edgings (both alike)

Work as for Front Opening, Hem and Hood Edging, attaching yarn at base of sleeve seam.

belt

With 5.00 mm (UK 6) hook and MS, make 7 ch.
1st row 1 dc into 2nd ch from hook, 1 dc into each dc to end, turn.
2nd row 1 ch (does not count as st), 1 dc into each dc to end, turn.
Rep last row until Belt measures 104 cm (41 in).
Fasten off.
Make thin basic tassels (see page 23), about 3 lengths each tassel, and attach to ends of belt.

✳ in the nursery

fab floor cushion

Big, bold and bright, this floor cushion is fun to make. The circles can be moved around to make your own pattern.

materials

11 50 g (1¾ oz) balls Rowan Cotton Glace in main shade (**MS**) Maritime 817; 1 50 g (1¾ oz) ball Rowan Cotton Glace in first contrast (**1st C**) Poppy 741; 1 50 g (1¾ oz) ball Rowan Cotton Glace in second contrast (**2nd C**) Bleached 726; 1 50 g (1¾ oz) ball Rowan Cotton Glace in third contrast (**3rd C**) Sky 749; and 1 50 g (1¾ oz) ball Rowan Cotton Glace in fourth contrast (**4th C**) Nightshade 746
3.00 mm (UK 11) crochet hook
Cushion pad 58 x 58 cm (22½ x 22½ in)
18 buttons

size

57 x 57 cm (2½ x 2½ in)

tension (gauge)

20 sts and 12 rows to 10 cm (4 in) measured over treble crochet worked with a 3.00 mm (UK 11) hook or the size required to achieve this tension.

abbreviations

beg beginning; **ch** chain; **cm** centimetre(s); **cont** continue; **in** inch(es); **mm** millimetre(s); **rem** remain(ing); **rep** repeat; **RS** right side; **ss** slip stitch; **st(s)** stitch(es); **tr** treble

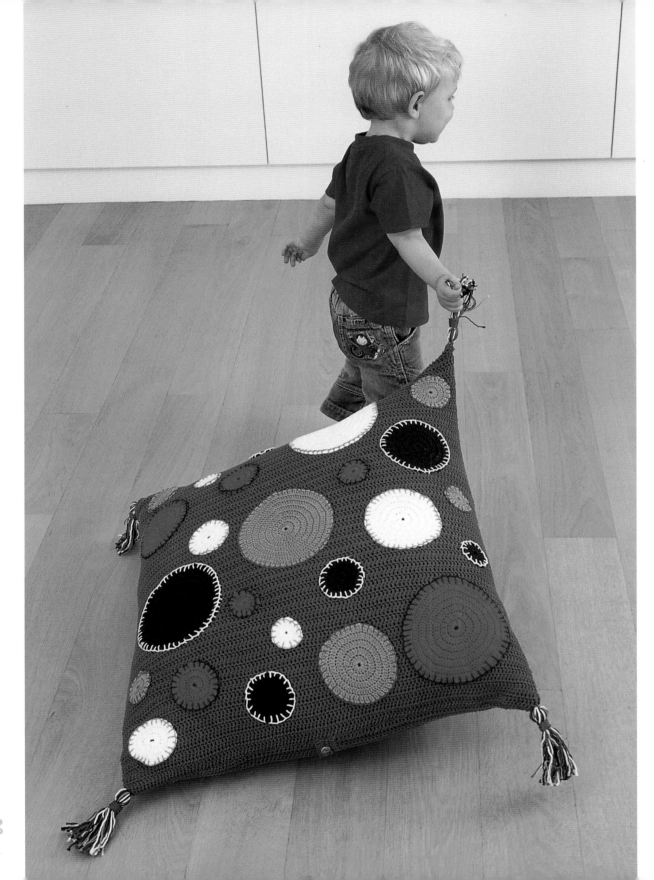

front

With 3.00 mm (UK 11) hook and MS, make 116 ch.
Foundation row 1 tr into 4th ch from hook, 1 tr into each ch to end, turn.
1st row (RS) 3 ch (counts as first st), miss first tr, 1 tr into each tr, ending 1 tr into 3rd of 3 ch, turn.
Rep 1st row until work measures 57 cm (22½ in).
Fasten off.

back (make 2)

With 3.00 mm (UK 11) hook and MS, make 58 ch.
Work as for Front until Back measures 57 cm (22½ in).
Fasten off.

to finish

With RS together, sew the 2 backs to the front leaving an opening down the centre of the back.

buttonhole band

With 3.00 mm (UK 11) hook and MS, rejoin yarn to centre back at one side.
1st row 3 ch, work tr evenly along opening to end, turn.
2nd row 3 ch (counts as first st), miss first tr, 1 tr into each tr to end, turn.
3rd row As 2nd row.
Fasten off.
Sew down buttonhole band at each end.

Sew 18 buttons down other side of back opening evenly spaced and using tr patt on buttonhole band to fasten.
Make 4 decorative tassels (see page 23) using all 5 colours of yarn and attach one to each corner.

basic circle

With 3.00 mm (UK 11) hook and 1st C, make 5 ch, ss into first ch to form a ring.
1st round 3 ch, 15 tr into ring, ss into 3rd of 3 ch at beg of round. (16 tr)
2nd round 3 ch, 1 tr in ch at base of these 3 ch, 2 tr in every tr, ss into 3rd of 3 ch at beg of round. (32 tr)
3rd round 3 ch, 2 tr in next tr, (1 tr in next tr, 2 tr in next tr) 15 times, ss into 3rd of 3 ch at beg of round. (48 tr)
4th round 3 ch, 2 tr in next tr, (1 tr in each of next 2 tr, 2 tr in next tr) 15 times, 1 tr in next tr, ss into 3rd of 3 ch at beg of round. (64 tr)
Cont in this way, working 16 extra tr in every round.
Make circles in 4 sizes: small = 2 rounds, medium = 3 rounds, large = 5 rounds and extra large = 7 rounds.
Make circles in every contrast colour in every size and make extra to fill in the gaps.
Place the circles randomly on the front of the cushion and use blanket stitch and a contrasting colour to sew them in place.

super storage pockets

This versatile hanging storage is perfect for keeping nursery essentials to hand or for providing a home for teddies and dolls.

materials

7 50 g (1¾ oz) balls Rowan All Seasons Cotton in main shade (**MS**) Citron 216; 1st Contrast 1 50 g (1¾ oz) ball Rowan All Seasons Cotton in first contrast (**1st C**) Lime Leaf 217; and 1 50 g (1¾ oz) ball Rowan Cashsoft Baby DK (for stars) in second contrast (**2nd C**) Limone 802
4.00 mm (UK 8) crochet hook
3.50 mm (UK 9) crochet hook
4 buttons
Cane about 40 cm (16 in) long

size

35 x 80 cm (14 x 31½ in)

tension (gauge)

15 sts and 10 rows to 10 cm (4 in) measured over treble crochet worked with a 4.00 mm (UK 8) hook or the size required to achieve this tension.

abbreviations

ch chain; **cm** centimetre(s); **dc** double crochet; **htr** half treble; **in** inch(es); **mm** millimetre(s); **rep** repeat; **ss** slip stitch; **st(s)** stitch(es); **tr** treble

base

With 4.00 mm (UK 8) hook and MS, make 53 ch.
1st row (RS) 1 tr into 4th ch from hook, 1 tr into each ch to end, turn. (51 sts)
2nd row 3 ch (counts as first tr), miss first tr, 1 tr into each tr to end, turn.
Rep 2nd row until work measures 80 cm (31½ in). Fasten off.

pockets (make 3)

With 4.00 mm (UK 8) hook and MS, make 33 ch.
1st row (RS) 1 tr into 4th ch from hook, 1 tr into each ch to end, turn. (31 sts)
2nd row 3 ch (counts as first tr), miss first tr, 1 tr into each tr to end, turn
Rep 2nd row until work measure 20 cm (8 in). Fasten off.

stars (make 11)

With 3.50 mm (UK 9) hook and 2nd C, make 6 ch, ss into first ch to form a ring.
1st round 1 ch, 18 dc into ring, ss into first dc.
2nd round 9 ch, 1 dc into 4th ch from hook, 1 htr into each next 2 ch, 1 tr into each next 3 ch, miss first

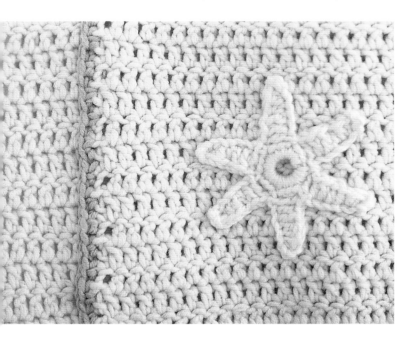

3 dc on ring, ss into next dc, *9 ch, 1 dc into 4th ch from hook, 1 htr into each next 2 ch, 1 tr into each next 3 ch, miss 2 dc on ring, ss into next dc, rep from * 4 more times, ending ss into ss on previous round. Fasten off.

tab tops (make 4)

With 4.00 mm (UK 8) hook and 1st C, make 22 ch.
Work 4 rows of dc.
Fasten off.

to finish

With 4.00 mm (UK 8) hook and 1st C, work 1 row of dc around the sides of base and all 3 pockets. Sew the pockets down the centre of base, spacing them evenly. Randomly sew the stars over the pockets and base (see the photograph as a guide).
Sew the tab tops along the top of the base, folding them in half and overlapping the base by 2 cm (¾ in).
Sew a button to each tab top.
Sew in any loose ends.
Put the length of cane through the tab tops.
Make a length of ch about 50 cm (20 in) long and tie it to both ends of the cane (this is optional for hanging up the pockets).

baby blanket

Worked in stripes using a soft and airy yarn, this is the perfect blanket for a newborn baby. Change colour every row for a more regular effect.

materials

3 50 g (1¼ oz) balls Rowan Soft Baby in main shade (**MS**) Angel 02; and 3 50 g (1¼ oz) balls Rowan Soft Baby in contrast (**C**) Cloud 01
4.50 mm (UK 7) crochet hook

size

70 x 94 cm (27 x 37 in)

tension (gauge)

16 sts and 9 rows to 10 cm (4 in) measured over treble crochet worked with a 4.50 mm (UK 7) hook or the size required to achieve this tension.

abbreviations

beg beginning; **ch** chain; **cm** centimetre(s); **cont** continue; **in** inch(es); **mm** millimetre(s); **patt** pattern; **rep** repeat(ing); **sp** space; **ss** slip stitch; **st(s)** stitch(es); **tr** treble

blanket

With 4.50 mm (UK 7) hook and MS, make 42 ch.

1st round 2 tr into 6th ch from hook, 1 tr in each ch to last ch, (2 tr, 2 ch, 3 tr, 2 ch, 2 tr) in last ch, work along lower edge of ch; 1 tr in each ch to ch containing 2 tr at beg, (2 tr, 2 ch, 2 tr) in this ch, 1 ss in 3rd of 5 ch at beg of round.

Change to C.

2nd round 1 ss in next ch, 5 ch, 2 tr under next ch, *1 tr in each tr to corner, (2 tr, 2 ch, 2 tr) in 2 ch sp, rep from * twice more, 1 tr in each tr, ending 1 tr in 3rd of 5 ch at beg of previous round, 1 tr under next ch, 1 ss in 3rd of 5 ch at beg of this round.

Cont rep 2nd round, working 4 extra tr on each side on every round and working stripe patt as follows.

Change to MS and work 1 round.
Change to C and work 1 round.
Change to MS and work 2 rounds.
Change to C and work 2 rounds.
Change to MS and work 2 rounds.
Change to C and work 2 rounds.
Change to MS and work 3 rounds.
Change to C and work 4 rounds.
Change to MS and work 1 round.
Change to C and work 3 rounds.
Change to MS and work 1 round.
Change to C and work 1 round.
Change to MS and work 2 rounds.
Fasten off.

to finish

Sew in any loose ends.

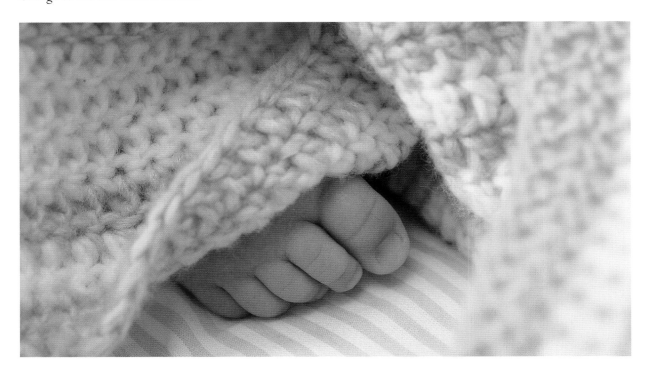

dress-up rag doll

Every little girl loves dolls, and this one comes with its own clothes and curly hair. Make extra clothing in bright colours for more dressing-up fun.

materials

2 50 g (1¾ oz) balls Rowan Cashsoft Baby DK in main shade (**MS**) Pixie 807; 1 50 g (1¾ oz) ball Rowan Cashsoft Baby DK in 1st contrast (**1st C**) Limone 802; 1 50 g (1¾ oz) ball Rowan Cashsoft Baby DK in 2nd contrast (**2nd C**) Glacier 504; and 1 50 g (1¾ oz) ball Rowan Cashsoft Baby DK in 3rd contrast (**3rd C**) Savannah 507
3.50 mm (UK 9) crochet hook
Oddments of yarn for the face
Stuffing
2 buttons
3 lengths of narrow ribbon

size

35 cm (14 in)

tension (gauge)

21 sts and 23 rows to 10 cm (4 in) measured over double crochet worked with a 3.50 mm (UK 9) hook or the size required to achieve this tension.

abbreviations

beg beginning; **ch** chain; **cm** centimetre(s); **cont** continue; **dc** double crochet; **dc2tog** (insert hook as indicated, yoh and draw loop through) twice, yoh and draw through all 3 loops on hook; **in** inch(es); **mm** millimetre(s); **rep** repeat; **ss** slip stitch; **st(s)** stitch(es); **tr** treble; **yoh** yarn over hook

head

With 3.50 mm (UK 9) hook and MS and starting at front of face, make 4 ch, ss into first ch to form a ring.

1st round 1 ch (does not count as first st), 2 dc into each st to end, ss into first dc. (8 sts)

2nd round 1 ch (does not count as first st), 2 dc into each dc to end, ss into first dc. (16 sts)

3rd round 1 ch (does not count as first st), (1 dc into next dc, 2 dc into next dc) 8 times, ss into first dc. (24 sts)

4th round 1 ch (does not count as first st), (1 dc into next dc, 2 dc into next dc) 12 times, ss into first dc. (36 sts)

5th round 1 ch (does not count as first st), 1 dc into each dc to end, ss into first dc.

Rep last round 3 times more.

9th round 1 ch (does not count as first st), (dc2tog over next 2 dc, 1 dc into next dc) 12 times, ss into first dc. (24 sts)

10th round 1 ch (does not count as first st), (dc2tog

over next 2 sts, 1 dc into next st) 8 times, ss into first dc. (16 sts)

11th round 1 ch (does not count as first st), (dc2tog over next 2 sts) 8 times, ss into first dc. (8 sts)

Stuff the head and carefully work the next round as follows.

12th round 1 ch (does not count as first st), (dc2tog) 4 times. (4 sts)

Fasten off and use the loose end to sew up the hole at the back of the head.

body

With 3.50 mm (UK 9) hook and MS and starting at bottom of body, make 4 ch, ss into first ch to form a ring.

1st round 1 ch (does not count as first st), 2 dc into each st to end, ss into first dc. (8 sts)

2nd round 1 ch (does not count as first st), 2 dc into each dc to end, ss into first dc. (16 sts)

3rd round 1 ch (does not count as first st), (2 dc into next st, 1 dc into next st) 8 times, ss into first dc. (24 sts)

4th round 1 ch (does not count as first st), 1 dc into each dc to end, ss into first dc.

Rep the last round until work measures 14 cm (5½ in).

Next round 1 ch (does not count as first st), (dc2tog over next 2 dc) 12 times, ss into first dc. (12 sts)

Stuff the body and carefully work the next 2 rounds as follows.

Next round 1 ch (does not count as first st), (dc2tog) 6 times, ss into first dc. (6 sts)

Next round 1 ch (does not count as first st), (dc2tog) 3 times, ss into first dc. (3 sts)

Fasten off and use the loose end to sew up the hole at the top of the body.

arm (make 2)

With 3.50 mm (UK 9) hook and MS, make 4 ch, ss into first ch to form a ring.

1st round 1 ch (does not count as first st), 2 dc into each st to end, ss into first dc. (8 sts)

2nd round 1 ch (does not count as first st), 1 dc into each dc to end, ss into first dc.

Rep last round until work measures 9 cm (3½ in).

Stuff the arm and work the last round as follows.

Next round 1 ch (does not count as first st), (dc2tog) 4 times, ss into first dc.

Fasten off and use the loose end to sew up the hole at the top of the arm.

leg (make 2)

With 3.50 mm (UK 9) hook and MS, make 4 ch, ss into first ch to form a ring.

1st round 1 ch, (does not count as first st), 2 dc into each st to end, ss into first dc. (8 sts)

2nd round 1 ch (does not count as first st), (2 dc into next dc, 1 dc into next dc) 4 times, ss into first dc. (12 sts)

3rd round 1 ch (does not count as first st), 1 dc into each dc to end, ss into first dc.

Rep 3rd round until work measures 12 cm (4¾ in). Stuff the leg and work the next 2 rounds carefully as follows.

Next round 1 ch (does not count as first st), (dc2tog) 6 times, ss into first dc. (6 sts)

Next round 1 ch (does not count as first st), (dc2tog) 3 times, ss into first dc. (3 sts)

Fasten off and use the loose end to sew up the top of the leg.

feet (make 2)

Work as leg to end of 3rd round.
Rep 3rd round until work measures 5 cm (2 in). Stuff the foot and work the last 2 rounds of leg.

skirt

With 3.50 mm (UK 9) hook and 1st C, make 30 ch.

1st row 1 tr into 4th ch from hook, 1 tr into each ch to end, turn. (28 sts)

2nd row 3 ch (counts as first tr), 1 tr into each tr to end, tr into top of turning ch, turn.

3rd row 3 ch (counts as first tr), 2 tr into next tr, 1 tr into each tr to last 2 sts, 2 tr into next tr, 1 tr into last tr, turn.

Rep 3rd row 3 more times. (36 sts)

7th row As 2nd row.

Rep 7th row until skirt measures 10 cm (4 in). Break off 1st C and join in 2nd C.

Next row 1 ch, 1 dc into each of first 2 tr, *3 ch, ss into first ch, 1 dc into each of next 2 tr, rep from * to end.

Fasten off.

waistcoat
back

With 3.50 mm (UK 9) hook and 2nd C, make 17 ch.

Foundation row 1 dc into 2nd ch from hook, 1 dc into each ch to end, turn.

1st row 3 ch, 1 tr into base of 3 ch, *miss 2 dc, 3 tr into next dc, rep from * to last 3 sts, miss 2 dc, 2 tr into last dc, turn.

2nd row 1 ch, 1 dc into first tr, *2 ch, miss 2 tr, 1 dc into next tr (centre of 3 tr), rep from * to last 3 sts, 2 ch, miss 2 tr, 1 dc into top of 3 ch, turn.

3rd row 3 ch, 1 tr into base of 3 ch, *miss 2 ch, 3 tr into next dc, rep from * to last 3 sts, miss 2 ch, 2 tr into last dc, turn.

Rep 2nd and 3rd rows until work measures 8 cm (3 in), ending with 3rd row.
Fasten off.

front (make 2)

With 3.50 mm (UK 9) hook and 2nd C, make 8 ch.
Work in patt as for back.

hair

With 3.50 mm (UK 9) hook, 3rd C, starting at side of the face and leaving a length of yarn about 6 cm (2½ in) at beg, work on head as follows: 1 dc into first dc on head, 5 ch, *1 dc into next dc on head, 5 ch, rep from * until you have worked over to the other side of the head. Fasten off, leaving a length of yarn about 6 cm (2½ in). Cont working from side to side over head, row after row, from front to back until you have a full head of hair. Unravel the lengths of hair at each side of face. Use 2 lengths of ribbon to tie a bow around the unravelled hair.

to finish

Sew together all body parts (see pages 20-21).
Sew up the skirt, making sure that the seam goes to the back. Thread a length of ribbon through the top of the skirt and tie it in a bow at the front.
Sew the shoulder and side seams of the waistcoat, leaving a 2 cm (¾ in) gap for armholes. Sew 2 buttons to the front of the waistcoat.
Stitch a face on the front of the head using oddments of colour and stitch fingers at end of arms.
Sew in any loose ends.

toy sack

If you're fed up with toys all over the floor have a go at making this bright and colourful toy sack to store them all away. It is quick and really easy to make.

materials

4 50 g (1¾ oz) balls Rowan Handknit DK Cotton in main shade (**MS**) Rosso 215; 4 50 g (1¾ oz) balls Rowan Handknit DK Cotton in 1st contrast (**1st C**) Flame 254; and 4 50 g (1¾ oz) balls Rowan Handknit DK Cotton in 2nd contrast (**2nd C**) Mango Fool 319
4.00 mm (UK 8) crochet hook

size

44 x 56 cm (17 x 22 in)

tension (gauge)

15 sts and 10 rows to 10 cm (4 in) measured over treble crochet worked with a 4.00 mm (UK 8) hook or the size required to achieve this tension.

abbreviations

beg beginning; **ch** chain; **cm** centimetre(s); **dc** double crochet; **in** inch(es); **mm** millimetre(s); **patt** pattern; **rep** repeat; **ss** slip stitch; **st(s)** stitch(es); **tr** treble

sack (worked in one piece)

With 4.00 mm (UK 8) hook and MS, make 132 ch, ss into first ch to form a ring.

1st round 3 ch (counts as first tr), 1 tr into each of next 6 sts, *(1 ch, miss 1 ch, 1 tr in next st) 3 times, 1 tr into each of next 6 sts, rep from * to last 5 sts, 1 ch, 1 tr, 1 ch, 1 tr, 1 ch into next 5 sts, ss into top of 3 ch at beg of round.

2nd round 3 ch (counts as first tr), 1 tr into each of next 6 tr, *(1 ch, miss 1 ch, 1 tr into next tr) 3 times, 1 tr into each of next 6 tr, rep from * to last 5 sts, 1 ch, 1 tr, 1 ch, 1 tr, 1 ch into next 5 sts, ss into top of 3 ch at beg of round.

3rd round As 2nd round.

4th round 4 ch (counts as 1 tr, 1 ch), miss first 2 tr, 1 tr into next tr, (1 ch, miss 1 tr, 1 tr into next tr) twice, *1 tr into each of next 6 sts, (1 ch, miss 1 tr, 1 tr into next tr) 3 times, rep from * to last 5 sts, 1 tr into each of next 5 sts, ss into top of 3 ch at beg of round.

5th round 4 ch (counts as 1 tr, 1 ch) (miss first tr and 1 ch), 1 tr into next tr, (1 ch, miss 1 ch, 1 tr into next tr) twice, *1 tr into each of next 6 tr, (1 ch, miss 1 ch, 1 tr in next tr) 3 times, rep from * to last 5 sts, 1 tr into each of next 5 tr, ss into top of 3 ch at beg of round.

6th round As 5th round.

These 6 rounds give a full rep of the patt.
Change to 1st C.
Work 1 full rep of the patt.
Change to 2nd C.
Work 1 full rep of the patt.
These 18 rows just worked give 1 full patt and colour rep. Work these 18 rows twice more.
Fasten off.

tie (make 2)

With 4.00 mm (UK 8) hook and MS, make 130 ch.
Work 1 row in dc.
Fasten off.

to finish

Sew across the bottom of the sack (see pages 20-21).
Sew in any loose ends.
Thread ties through top of sack, 1 block down, weaving in and out of holes in patt. Sew ends of ties together.
Pull one tie to the left and the other to the right to form drawstrings.
Make basic tassels (see page 23) and attach them to the bottom of the sack.

spiral rug

This bright and colourful rug can be made for any room. Change the colours to match your decor or add extra rounds to make it bigger.

materials

5 50 g (1¾ oz) balls Rowan Cotton Rope in main shade (**MS**) Lemonade 060; 5 50 g (1¾ oz) balls Rowan Cotton Rope in 1st contrast (**1st C**) Limeade 065; and 5 50 g (1¾ oz) balls Rowan Cotton Rope in 2nd contrast (**2nd C**) Calypso 064
7.00 mm (UK 2) crochet hook

size

71 cm (28 in) across

tension (gauge)

9 sts and 4¼ rows to 10 cm (4 in) measured over treble crochet worked with a 7.00 mm (UK 2) hook using 2 ends of yarn or the size required to achieve this tension.

abbreviations

beg beginning; **ch** chain; **cm** centimetre(s); **cont** continue; **in** inch(es); **mm** millimetre(s); **patt** pattern; **ss** slip stitch; **st(s)** stitch(es); **tr** treble

note

Use 2 ends of yarn throughout and work into the back of each stitch in every round.

rug

With 7.00 mm (UK 2) hook and MS, make 5 ch, ss into first ch to form a ring.

1st round 3 ch, 15 tr into ring, ss into 3rd of 3 ch at beg of round. (16 tr)
Change to 1st C.

2nd round 3 ch, 1 tr in ch at base of these 3 ch, 2 tr in every tr, ss into 3rd of 3 ch at beg of round. (32 tr)
Change to 2nd C.

3rd round 3 ch, 2 tr into next tr, (1 tr into next tr, 2 tr into next tr) 15 times, ss into 3rd of 3 ch at beg of round. (48 tr)
Change to MS.

4th round 3 ch, 2 tr into next tr, (1 tr into each of next 2 tr, 2 tr into next tr) 15 times, 1 tr into next tr, ss into 3rd of 3 ch at beg of round. (64 tr)
Change to 1st C.

5th round 3 ch, 2 tr into next tr, (1 tr into each of next 3 tr, 2 tr into next tr) 15 times, 1 tr into each of next 2 tr, ss into 3rd of 3 ch at beg of round. (80 sts)
Change to 2nd C.

6th round 3 ch, 2 tr into next tr, (1 tr into each of next 4 tr, 2 tr into next tr) 15 times, 1 tr into each of next 3 tr, ss into 3rd of 3 ch at beg of round. (96 sts)
Cont in stripe patt and working 16 extra sts on every round until rug measures 71 cm (28 in) or 15 rounds have been worked.
Fasten off.

to finish

Sew in any loose ends.

cushy cushion

This pretty cushion is made in one piece by joining each square as you work so there's no sewing up afterwards. Small buttons trim the back.

materials

5 50 g (1¾ oz) balls Rowan 4-ply soft in Wink 377
3.00 mm (UK 11) crochet hook
16 small beads or buttons
30 cm (12 in) pad cushion

size

32 x 32 cm (12½ x 12½ in)

tension (gauge)

Each square measures 8 x 8 cm (3 x 3 in) worked with a 3.00 mm (UK 11) hook or the size required to achieve this tension.

abbreviations

beg beginning; **ch** chain; **cm** centimetre(s); **cont** continue; **dc** double crochet; **in** inch(es); **mm** millimetre(s); **picot** 3 ch, ss into side of last dc worked; **rep** repeat; **sp** space(s); **ss** slip stitch; **tr** treble

cushion (worked in one piece)
first square

With 3.00 mm (UK 11) hook, make 6 ch, ss into first ch to form a ring.

1st round 3 ch (counts as first tr), work 15 tr into ring, ss into 3rd of 3 ch at beg of round.

2nd round 5 ch (counts as 1 tr, 2 ch), (1 tr into next tr, 2 ch) 15 times, ss into 3rd of 5 ch at beg of round.

3rd round ss into first 2 ch sp, 3 ch (counts as 1 tr), work 2 tr into first 2 ch sp, 1 ch, (3 tr into next 2 ch sp, 1 ch) 15 times, ss into 3rd of 3 ch at beg of round.

4th round ss into each of next 2 tr, 1 ch, 1 dc into first ch sp, 3 ch, 1 dc into next ch sp, 6 ch, *1 dc into next ch sp, (3 ch, 1 dc into next ch sp) 3 times, 6 ch, rep from * twice more, (1 dc into next ch sp, 3 ch) twice, ss into first dc.

5th round ss into first 3 ch sp, 3 ch, work 2 tr into first 3 ch sp, into next 6 ch arch work (5 tr, 2 ch, 5 tr), * 3 tr into each of next 3 3 ch sp, into next 6 ch arch work (5 tr, 2 ch, 5 tr), rep from * twice more, 3 tr into each of last 2 3 ch sp, ss into 3rd of 3 ch at beg of round.

6th round 1 ch, 1 dc into same st as last ss, 1 dc into each of next 2 tr, 1 picot, 1 dc into each of next 5 tr, into next 2 ch sp work (1 dc, 1 picot, 1 dc), 1 dc into each of next 5 tr, *1 picot, (1 dc into each of next 3 tr, 1 picot) 3 times, 1 dc into each of next 5 tr, into next 2 ch sp work (1 dc, 1 picot, 1 dc), 1 dc into each of next 5 tr, rep from * twice more, 1 picot, (1 dc into each of next 3 tr, 1 picot) twice, ss into first dc. Fasten off.

Cont making squares as above but on the 6th round, to join a square to another square, instead of a picot work 1 ch, 1 dc into picot on other square, 1 ch, making sure that you join all 4 picots down the side of the square and the 2 corner picots.

Join 16 squares together for front.

Join 8 squares down one side of the back also joining squares at either end to corresponding squares of front and 8 squares down the other side, leaving an opening down the centre and making sure that when you make the centre squares you have picots on each square.

to finish

Sew beads or buttons one side of the opening. Use the picots on the other side as buttonholes.

floppity teddy

No child's toy box is complete without a special teddy. Adorned with his very own scarf, this teddy is certain to be a favourite companion.

materials

2 50 g (1¾ oz) balls Rowan Cashsoft DK in main shade (**MS**) Savannah 507; 1 50 g (1¾ oz) ball Rowan Cashsoft DK in 1st contrast (**1st C**) Donkey 517; 1 50 g (1¾ oz) ball Rowan Cashsoft DK in 2nd contrast (**2nd C**) Clementine 510; 1 50 g (1¾ oz) ball Rowan Cashsoft DK in 3rd contrast (**3rd C**) Madame 511; 1 50 g (1¾ oz) ball Rowan Cashsoft DK in 4th contrast (**4th C**) Lime 509; and 1 50 g (1¾ oz) ball Rowan Cashsoft DK in 5th contrast (**5th C**) Ballad Blue 508
3.50 mm (UK 9) crochet hook
Stuffing
Oddments of yarn for face
4 buttons

size

31 cm (12 in)

tension (gauge)

21 sts and 23 rows to 10 cm (4 in) measured over double crochet worked with a 3.50 mm (UK 9) hook or the size required to achieve this tension.

abbreviations

ch chain; **cm** centimetre(s); **cont** continue; **dc** double crochet; **dc2tog** (insert hook as indicated, yoh and draw loop through) twice, yoh and draw through all 3 loops on hook; **in** inch(es); **mm** millimetre(s); **rem** remain(ing); **rep** repeat; **st(s)** stitch(es); **yoh** yarn over hook

head (make 2)

With 3.50 mm (UK 9) hook and MS and starting at neck, make 9 ch.

Foundation row 1 dc into 2nd ch from hook, 1 dc into each ch to end, turn.

1st row 1 ch (does not count as first st), 2 dc into first dc, 1 dc into each dc to last dc, 2 dc into last dc, turn.

2nd row 1 ch (does not count as first st), 1 dc into each dc to end, turn.

Rep 1st and 2nd until work measures 6 cm (2½ in).

Next row As 2nd row.

Cont working 2nd row until work measures 10 cm (4 in).

Fasten off.

body (make 2)

With 3.50 mm (UK 9) hook and MS and starting at neck edge and working downwards, make 13 ch.

Foundation row 1 dc into 2nd ch from hook, 1 dc into each ch to end, turn.

1st row 1 ch (does not count as first st), 2 dc into first dc, 1 dc into each dc to last dc, 2 dc into last dc, turn.

Rep 1st row 4 more times.

Next row 1 ch (does not count as first st), 1 dc into each dc to end, turn.

Cont working last row until work measures 14 cm (5½ in).

Fasten off.

leg (make 4)

With 3.50 mm (UK 9) hook and MS and starting at sole of foot, make 13 ch.

Foundation row 1 dc into 2nd ch from hook, 1 dc into each ch to end, turn.

1st row 1 ch (does not count as first st), 1 dc into each dc to end, turn.

Rep 1st row 4 more times.

6th row 1 ch (does not count as first st) 1 dc into each of next 6 dc, turn, leaving rem sts unworked.

Rep 6th row 14 more times.

Fasten off.

arm (make 2)

With 3.50 mm (UK 9) hook and MS, make 20 ch.

Foundation row 1 dc into 2nd ch from hook, 1 dc into each ch to end, turn.

1st row 1 ch (does not count as first st), 1 dc into each dc to end, turn.

Rep 1st row 11 times more.

Fasten off.

ear (make 2)

With 3.50 mm (UK 9) hook and 1st C, make 5 ch.

Foundation row 1 dc into 2nd ch from hook, 1 dc into each ch to end, turn.

1st row 1 ch (does not count as first st), 1 dc into each dc to end, turn.

Rep 1st row 9 times more.

11th row (dc2tog) twice, turn.

12th row dc2tog.

Fasten off.

to finish

Sew in loose ends.

With RS together, sew around head, leaving a small opening for stuffing. Turn right side out and stuff. Sew up the opening.

Do the same with the body, legs and arms, making sure that when you sew the legs together you round off the heel and toes on the foot.

Sew ears to the top of the head.

With oddments of yarn and 1st C, sew facial features on the head and claws at the ends of arms (see photograph as a guide).

Sew 4 buttons down the centre of the body.

scarf

With 3.50 mm (UK 9) hook and 2nd C, make 7 ch.

Foundation row 1 dc into 2nd ch from hook, 1 dc into each ch to end, turn.

Next row 1 ch (does not count as first st), 1 dc into each dc to end, turn.

Rep the last row throughout and change colour every 8th row until scarf measures about 40 cm (15¾ in), finishing with a full rep of a colour.

Sew in loose ends.

hanging motifs

These decorative motifs can be made in different colours to suit any room. Try filling them with dried lavender to create a relaxing atmosphere.

materials

1 50 g (1¾ oz) ball Rowan 4-ply Soft in main shade (**MS**) Wink 377; and
1 50 g (1¾ oz) ball Rowan 4-ply Soft in contrast (**C**) Honk 374
3.00 mm (UK 11) crochet hook
Beads and sequins to match colours of motifs
Stuffing

sizes

Flower motif 7 cm (2¾ in), heart motif 5 cm (2 in)

tension (gauge)

22 sts and 18 rows to 10 cm (4 in) measured over treble crochet worked with a 3.00 mm (UK 11) hook or the size required to achieve this tension.

abbreviations

beg beginning; **ch** chain; **cm** centimetre(s); **dc** double crochet; **htr** half treble; **in** inch(es); **mm** millimetre(s); **rep** repeat; **ss** slip stitch; **st(s)** stitch(es); **tr** treble

flower (make 2)

With 3.00 mm (UK 11) hook and MS, make 6 ch, ss into first ch to form a ring.

1st round 1 ch, 18 dc into ring, ss into first dc.

2nd round 9 ch, 1 dc into 4th ch from hook, 1 htr into each of next 2 ch, 1 tr into each of next 3 ch, miss first 3 dc on ring, ss into next dc, *9 ch, 1 dc into 4th ch from hook, 1 htr into each of next 2 ch, 1 tr into each of next 3 ch, miss next 2 dc on ring, ss into next dc, rep from * 4 more times, ending ss into ss on previous round.

3rd round Work 1 row of dc around all edges of flower, working 3 dc into top of every point.

Fasten off.

heart (make 2)

With 3.00 mm (UK 11) hook and C, make 6 ch, ss into first ch sp to form a ring.

1st round 3 ch (counts as first tr), 16 tr into ring, ss into 3rd of 3 ch at beg of round. (17 sts)

2nd round 3 ch (counts as first tr), 1 tr into base of 3 ch, 2 tr into each tr to end, ss into 3rd of 3 ch at beg of round. (34 sts)

3rd round 1 ch (does not count as first st), 1 dc into first st, 3 tr into next st, 2 tr into each of next 4 sts, 1 htr into each of next 9 sts, 1 dc into each of next 4 sts, 1 htr into each of next 9 sts, 2 tr into each of next 4 sts, 3 tr into next st, 1 dc into last st, ss into ch at beg of round.

Fasten off.

to finish (both motifs)

With RS facing, sew around the shape, leaving an opening, turn RS out and stuff each motif. Sew up the opening. Decorate each motif with beads and sequins. Using 2 lengths of MS and 2 of C, make a twisted cord, about 110 cm (43 in) long, for hanging motifs. With 3.00 mm (UK 11) hook and colour to match each motif, make 16 ch, leaving a length of yarn each end of chain to sew on to motifs. Sew the chain in a loop to back of motifs. Thread the motifs on the twisted cord and hang up.

snuggle blanket

Made in soft yarn, this is the perfect comforter to help babies drift off to sleep. A perfect gift to give the mother of a newborn baby.

materials

2 50 g (1¾ oz) balls Rowan Wool Cotton in main shade (**MS**) Antique 900; 2 50 g (1¾ oz) balls Rowan Wool Cotton in first contrast (**1st C**) Hiss 952; and 2 50 g (1¾ oz) balls Rowan Wool Cotton in second contrast (**2nd C**) Tender 951
3.50 mm (UK 9) crochet hook

size

42 x 58 cm (16½ x 22¾ in), excluding edging

tension (gauge)

25 sts and 11 rows to 10 cm (4 in) measured over shell patt worked with a 3.50 mm (UK 9) hook or the size required to achieve this tension.

abbreviations

ch chain; **cm** centimetre(s); **dc** double crochet; **in** inch(es); **mm** millimetre(s); **patt** pattern; **rep** repeat; **RS** right side; **sp** space(s); **st(s)** stitch(es); **tr** treble(s); **tr3tog** work 1 tr into each of next 3 sts until 1 loop of each remains on hook, yoh and through all 4 loops on hook; **tr6tog** work 1 tr into each of next 6 sts until 1 loop of each remains on hook, yoh and through all 7 loops on hook; **yoh** yarn over hook

blanket

With 3.50 mm (UK 9) hook and MS, make 113 ch.
Foundation row (3 tr, 1 ch, 3 tr) into 5th ch from hook, miss 3 ch, 1 dc into next ch, *miss 3 ch, (3 tr, 1 ch, 3 tr) in next ch, miss 3 ch, 1 dc in next ch, rep from * to end, turn.
Change to 1st C.
1st row 3 ch, miss first dc, tr3tog over next 3 tr, *7 ch, miss 1 ch, tr6tog over next 6 tr (leaving 1 dc between groups unworked), rep from *, ending 7 ch, tr3tog over last 3 tr, 1 tr in 1 ch, turn.
2nd row 3 ch, miss first tr, 3 tr in top of tr3tog, *1 dc in 1 ch sp between tr 1 row below (enclosing centre of 7 ch), (3 tr, 1 ch, 3 tr) in top of tr6tog, rep from *, ending 3 tr in top of tr3tog, 1 tr in 3rd of 3 ch, turn.
Change to 2nd C.
3rd row 4 ch, miss first tr, *tr6tog over next 6 tr (leaving 1 dc between groups unworked), 7 ch, miss 1 ch, rep from *, ending 3 ch, 1 dc in 3rd of 3 ch, turn.
4th row 1 ch, miss first dc and 3 ch, *(3tr, 1 ch, 3 tr)

in top of tr6tog, 1 dc in 1 ch sp between tr 1 row below (enclosing centre of 7 ch), rep from *, ending 1 dc in first of 4 ch, turn.
Change to MS.
Rep 1st to 4th rows, changing colours every 2 rows until work measures 58 cm (22¾ in) and ending with MS on 3rd and 4th rows to give a full shell rep. Do not break yarn.

to finish

Work a row of shells evenly down the side of the blanket as 4th row, across the bottom (making sure that the sts match the shell patt from the foundation row) and up the other side.
Fasten off.
Sew in any loose ends.

index